THE WHITLAM MOB

MUNGO MacCALLUM

THE

WHITLAM MOB

Black Inc.

Published by Black Inc.,
an imprint of Schwartz Publishing Pty Ltd
37–39 Langridge Street
Collingwood VIC 3066 Australia
email: enquiries@blackincbooks.com
http://www.blackincbooks.com

The National Library of Australia Cataloguing-in-Publication entry:

MacCallum, Mungo (Mungo Wentworth), 1941- author.
The Whitlam mob / Mungo MacCallum.
9781863956796 (paperback)
9781922231758 (ebook)

Whitlam, Gough, 1916- Australian Labor Party--History--20th century.
Prime ministers--Australia.   Politicians--Australia.
Australia--Politics and government--1972-1975.
320.994

CONTENTS

THE OTHER MOB

PROLOGUE

Bliss was it in that dawn to be alive,
But to be young was very heaven!
WILLIAM WORDSWORTH

S O WROTE THE NAIVE BUT IDEALISTIC POET OF THE outbreak of the French Revolution in 1789, and it is fair to say that a lot of us felt much the same way on 3 December 1972. We may not have stormed the Bastille, but after twenty-three years of conservative rule the sense of liberation, of having triumphed over almost insuperable odds, was nearly as exhilarating.

We were perfectly aware that our heaven would not be nirvana – endless peace and contentment were not part of the deal. On the contrary, we remained bound tightly to the wheel, to the relentless program set down over many years by our own great revolutionary leader, Edward Gough

Whitlam. Implementing our own version of liberty, equality and fraternity would be neither swift nor simple. But at least we could be fairly certain that it would be managed without the terror and bloodshed that eventually made even such placid souls as Wordsworth question their initial embrace of the First Republic.

We were a motley mob, we *sans-culottes* of Canberra. Whitlam's parliamentary team had plenty of young hopefuls in it – the 1969 election in particular had brought an influx of bright young men eager to take on the world. And of course there were the old stagers, those who had soldiered through the tough times in opposition and believed that now their time had come. They were not about to make way for those they saw as blow-ins, yet to prove themselves in the furnace. Just two of them – Kim Beazley and Fred Daly – had been in parliament when Labor had last occupied the Treasury benches, but of course neither had been a minister. In this regard, the Whitlam mob were a bunch of neophytes.

And then there were the fringe dwellers and hangers-on, the ambitious and sometimes visionary public servants like Stephen Fitzgerald, Peter Wilenski, John Mant and others, who had been sweating on the day they might have political masters willing to listen to their own dreams of a new Australia. They were joined by a coterie of academics, mainly from the Australian National University, many of them with even more extravagant fantasies for the future. And there were the journalists, many openly wedded to the Whitlam cause, who waited impatiently, but also somewhat apprehensively, for the spate of headlines that were certain to ensue.

A number of them, some immediately, others later, actually became part of the government, ostensibly advising their student ministers, but often more intent upon becoming players in their own right. Among the most prominent were Eric Walsh, John Edwards, Tom Connors, David Solomon, George Negus, John Stubbs and Megan Stoyles. Others such as myself remained active in the press gallery, but were still obviously supportive of what almost all accepted was a long-overdue change of government. Not unjustifiably, the conservative opposition felt it was not getting equal treatment. But it could be said that, in the circumstances, it hardly merited it. All the action was on the government side.

The other mob may have felt neglected, but they remained defiant; after all those years, many conservatives saw themselves as divinely ordained for government. The election had been an extraordinary aberration, a temporary suspension of natural law, and time would shortly restore the balance. But they were not all like the French Bourbons: some at least were capable of learning. There was a young guard, headed by Andrew Peacock and Don Chipp, who could even be called progressive. The new opposition leader, Billy Snedden, was a likeable enough middle-roader, and for a while at least the party seemed willing to follow his moderate path.

In time, of course, the recalcitrants resumed control, but in those first heady days it seemed that Harold Holt and John Gorton, rather than the unfortunate throwback of Billy McMahon, might provide the model for the future. And certainly the principals, those who had cast themselves as the prophets of the new order, were so busy revelling in the

3

spoils of victory that they scarcely spared a thought for the obstacles that lay ahead, whether merely parliamentary or embodied in the entire social and economic structure. Throwing caution to the winds, they set out to force the *Queen Mary* into a U-turn on a sixpence.

I was never a direct participant, but I was a passionately keen observer of the whole process, counting many of the star players from both sides among my close acquaintances, and in some instances as personal friends. This book is a nostalgic reminiscence of those days of glory and disaster, of high drama and low farce. It is an attempt to come to grips with, in particular, the Whitlam mob: who they were, what they did, and how and why they did it.

THE WHITLAM MOB

GOUGH WHITLAM

OUGH WHITLAM MAY HAVE TAKEN GREAT DELIGHT IN designing his own funeral arrangements – or at least a self-mocking fantasy version of them. But the pleasure of reciting his epitaph rested with a colleague, the acerbic New South Wales premier Neville Wran, although in all probability it was penned by the great speechwriter Graham Freudenberg, who acted as an amanuensis to both men.

As Wran put it, 'It was said of Caesar Augustus that he found a Rome of brick and left it of marble. It can be said of Gough Whitlam that he found Sydney, Melbourne and Brisbane unsewered, and left them fully flushed.' It was a line that delighted the elder statesman, whose epic visions – national, international and, some believed, interplanetary – had their origins in a firmly grounded policy of improving the quality of life: he began with the outhouse, and reached for the sky.

It is for this breadth of vision, for the unquenchable optimism of his ambition, that Australia's twenty-first prime minister will be best remembered. He spent less than three years in office – less than a full constitutional term, although he won two elections in the process. But in Australian history his name outshines most of his predecessors; only Menzies and perhaps Deakin among the conservatives and Curtin and Chifley on the Labor side are similarly household names.

Edward Gough Whitlam truly became a legend in his own lifetime. But it was a different legend to different audiences. Most of the left saw him as a flawed genius and a political martyr well on the way to beatification, if not canonisation. The right regarded him as a monstrous aberration, a devilish warning to budding politicians of the awful fate that awaits those who overreach. All, however, acknowledged that he was the dominant figure of his times, a giant who bestrode the parliament in a way that few had done before him and none has approached since.

His achievements – the now legendary Program – were many and radical. Some, like Medicare (son of Medibank), consumer protection laws, the Family Court and of course the sewering of the outer suburbs, have endured. Others, like free university degrees, Aboriginal land rights, the Australian Assistance Plan (a scheme of grants to kick-start overdue projects in disadvantaged electorates) and the promotion of the arts as a national objective, have been axed, abandoned or severely watered down by his successors. But few would deny that the fall-out from the great social explosion of the Whitlam years is still spreading: Whitlam remains one of our few leaders who can be truly said to have changed Australia – not just for the brief period of his administration, but forever.

But change brings with it instability and insecurity, and the dark side of Whitlam's legacy is that the cost of trying to implement a grand political and social vision is now seen to be unacceptably high. The runaway inflation, high interest rates and burgeoning unemployment of the latter half of Whitlam's turbulent administration were not entirely his fault; the twin oil-price shocks of the early '70s caught every government in the world by surprise, and all, with the possible exception of the Japanese, failed to provide an adequate response. But Whitlam seemed unwilling even to try: when he did make a grand economic gesture in the form of an across-the-board tariff cut, the cure, in the short term, turned out to be worse than the disease.

Economics was never his strong suit; it was something for others to worry about while he got on with implementing The Program. The trouble was that none of his colleagues knew very much either, and they were highly suspicious of the better-informed Treasury officials, most of whom they saw as leftover conservatives dedicated to subverting The Program.

As was his wont, Whitlam was determined to crash through or crash, and while there may be argument about how effective he was in terms of implementing his own policy, there can be no doubt that the economy suffered collateral damage in the process, damage which was ultimately to prove fatal to the government. Thus, all his successors in the Labor leadership – Hayden, Hawke, Keating, Beazley, Crean, Latham, Rudd, Gillard and Shorten – have had to live under the shadow of Whitlam's supposed economic irresponsibility. The idea has since been refined into the great conservative lie that, whatever else happens, Labor is never really to be trusted with your money.

This doleful refrain, repeated at every election since 1975, is what the Tories would like to see engraved on Whitlam's tomb: they would prefer to see his brand of carefree exuberance, the daring and ambition of those years, buried and forgotten. If people must have aspirations, let them confine them to their own backyards: let them wish for bigger cars, more prestigious schools, perhaps a holiday home.

Let them not dream of making real changes to society, let alone to the world; the upheavals can be too great, the triumphs too destabilising, the disappointments too crushing. Let them remain relaxed and comfortable, but just a little fearful of those who would shake their complacency. This mantra makes perfect political sense; it won John Howard four elections and even put Tony Abbott, a man once thought to be unelectable, into the Lodge.

And yet, and yet. Somehow the grandeur of Whitlam lingers on, even among the under-forties, the generation that has only heard the stories and never experienced the high-wire act that was the reality. Somehow this unlikely figure, the Canberra-reared son of a public servant, the physically awkward, pedantic, legalistic, frequently self-righteous, often maddening and at times just plain boring preacher of reform, has become part of the Australian pantheon.

In part, of course, it is because he made his own myths. Much of what the public saw as Whitlam's bombast was in fact a somewhat clumsy attempt at self-deprecation. Like King Canute, he thrived on flattery but did not take it too seriously, and his attempts to put his flatterers in their place were often misunderstood.

In retrospect it is easy to see how. On one celebrated occasion, the director of the National Gallery of Australia, Betty Churcher, informed Whitlam of a plan – fortunately kyboshed – to make him appear to walk across water to the opening of an exhibition. 'Comrade,' Whitlam replied, 'that would not have been possible – the stigmata have not yet healed.' His fans found this hilarious but it confirmed the worst fears of his critics. Here was Whitlam literally challenging the Almighty. But of course he wasn't: Whitlam, though an agnostic, once described himself as a fellow traveller with Christianity and was a great respecter of religious belief. Rather than blaspheming, he was thumbing his nose, yet again, at the pretension, the pomposity and the hypocrisy of an establishment which all too frequently, in his view, failed to distinguish between God and Mammon. If the snobs didn't get the joke, that was their tough luck.

But he was certainly no prude; indeed, there were times when he could be positively prurient. I treasure the memory of a VIP flight in 1970, which was diverted from Melbourne to Hobart by bad weather. The travelling press corps was seriously miffed; most of us had already made more or less sybaritic arrangements for the forthcoming evening, instead of which we were now to be deposited in the bleak south. The prospect was made worse by the memory of a former Whitlam visit, during which the Labor leader had been accosted by an eager young reporter with the demand: 'Mr Whitlam, tell us what you will do for Tasmania.' Whitlam had replied with devastating honesty: 'What can I do for Tasmania – what can anybody do for Tasmania? I mean, the place is fucked.' There was a feeling that a return visit might not be entirely welcome. But this time Whitlam had words of optimism. 'There's one thing about Tasmania,' he reassured us. 'With all that inbreeding, there's always a chance of a bit of double-headed fellatio.' The trip was made.

I first met Gough Whitlam in 1969, shortly after I arrived in Canberra. I had seen him in action often enough, and been impressed by his oratory and his knowledge, but like many on the left I was not yet entirely sure where he stood on the key issues of the time, especially the war in Vietnam. As the heir to Arthur Calwell's noble but doomed anti-war crusade of 1966, Whitlam, while clearly determined to negotiate Australia's way out of the mess to our north, seemed to me not to have the same fire in his belly.

Although he had only been opposition leader for two years, he had already survived a challenge from the charismatic king of the streets, Jim Cairns (masterminded, oddly, by the man who claimed to be Whitlam's greatest admirer, Phillip Adams), and was clearly distrusted by some in his own party, notably the leader of the New South Wales Left, Lionel Murphy, with whom I felt considerable rapport.

Moreover, he was supported by the New South Wales Right, which even in those days was pretty awful. I realised later that the perception that Whitlam was on the right of the party, like the idea that Calwell was on the left, was no more than an accident of geography. Whitlam, the internationalist free-thinker, was bound to his dominant state faction, just as Calwell, the conservative Catholic advocate of White Australia, was bound to his. But at the time I was inclined to be suspicious of the smooth-talking lawyer who, like me, had benefited (or otherwise) from a cosseted childhood and a privileged education.

Our first meeting changed my mind completely; I was won over to lifelong Whitlamolatry. In place of the sinister manipulator I had half-expected, I found an amiable, funny and rather shy man desperately eager to explain his plans to transform Australia from the smug backwater of the Menzies years into a model for the rest of the world. In those days, the idea that Australia could take a leading role in any field other than sport was breathtaking, yet Whitlam seemed to believe that it was entirely possible, provided a meticulously prepared program of public education and overdue social change could be carried out – and, listening to him outline it thirty-five years ago, there seemed no good reason why it should not. Certainly, in the rapidly changing times of the late '60s, it was a cause worth embracing, and embrace it I did.

But I also embraced the man himself. While Whitlam, like Menzies, did not suffer fools gladly, he was not an intellectual snob; he was genuinely interested and concerned about people, not just en masse but as individuals. He took a personal interest in their affairs. When two opposition staffers married in Canberra in 1972, Whitlam interrupted a frantically busy election schedule to fly from Sydney to attend the ceremony. It was winter and Canberra airport was fogbound for several hours; his VIP aircraft could not land, but rather than return to Sydney, Whitlam waited until the weather cleared and made a belated appearance at the reception.

He became a secular godparent to one of my daughters, invited my extended family to the Lodge for a head-wetting, and maintained an interest in her welfare thereafter. He kept in touch with a huge round of colleagues, acquaintances and their families and was constantly performing small acts of kindness, although these too were frequently misconstrued by cynics. Once, after he had paid a private hospital visit to the child of a colleague, he was greatly distressed when an enemy put it about that he was just chasing an extra vote in caucus. The fact was much simpler: the boy had asked to meet his hero, and Whitlam, being a kind and generous human being, had obliged.

He was both a humanitarian and a humanist; he truly believed that if people were told the truth, were shown the possibilities for their future and given a genuine choice, they would behave sensibly, decently and even altruistically. In spite of repeated disappointments, he never lost that faith in people. It was this above all that made him such an attractive human being.

For his part, Whitlam seemed pleased to welcome onboard another class traitor, especially one who was both a scion of the Wentworth dynasty and a godson of Guy Harriott, the arch-Tory editor of the *Sydney Morning Herald*. The fact that I could recognise most of his classical allusions, even the ones in Latin, probably helped too. In those days the office of the leader of the opposition was a small and open affair: two advisers, a press secretary-cum-speechwriter, an appointments secretary and a stenographer (indeed, the prime minister's was not much bigger, although at least he had a separate press office). Whitlam's anteroom, to give the cramped area between the front door and his own hideaway a rather grander name than it deserved, was a favourite after-hours drinking spot for sympathetic members of the press gallery, of whom there was a growing number. The Leader, as he preferred to be called, seldom joined them in person, but his aura was always present; although it was more than three years before the slogan 'It's Time' was coined, the mood for change was already manifest.

But so were the many obstacles to it. While Whitlam was clearly on top of John Gorton in parliament and was already spoken of as an alternative prime minister, he had far outstripped the rest of his party as a thinker and a performer. He was starting to look like a winner, a concept which had become so unfamiliar to most of his followers as to be incomprehensible, almost unwelcome. Repeated defeats had drained the old guard of any real hope of victory; at times they seemed actually to fear the mere prospect of it. The right was content to bicker over the spoils of defeat, and the left had become obsessed with a model of socialist purity long past its use-by date. In vain did Whitlam remind them that politics was about power; the impotent, he jibed, were always pure. The apparatchiks, locked in vendettas that at times appeared positively Balkan, refused to give an inch.

Whitlam, with the help of the party's British-born secretary, Cyril Wyndham, had made some small inroads: at least the parliamentary leadership was now represented at the party's peak policy meetings. But such setbacks merely made the hard men of the left more determined to hang on to what they had kept. By the end of 1969 it was clear that not only was the party machine desperately in need of modernisation, but that it would be very hard for Whitlam to win an election unless this could be achieved.

Even so, he ran it desperately close. The swing to Labor in 1969 was almost 7 per cent and the party won seventeen seats – for a wondrous half-hour or so, it appeared that Labor had actually won, a prospect that filled the more level-headed with momentary dread. But the result also confirmed the problem. Victoria, the jewel in the Liberal crown and the last bastion of the Labor Left, refused to join in the fun. Once again, Whitlam declared war on those he saw as the recalcitrants on his own side. And in the end he won, with a little help from some rather unlikely allies, including Clyde Cameron, an old-fashioned socialist who had once bitterly opposed him on everything from state aid to the ANZUS treaty.

The promise of the ultimate reward – the labour ministry – persuaded Cameron and his faction to swap sides, giving Whitlam and his allies the extra votes they needed to secure federal intervention in Victoria. And so, well before the election of 1972, the Labor Party was dragged, at least temporarily, into the second half of the twentieth century. The old Labor policies, including the pledge of nationalisation, which Whitlam described as the Old Testament, had been superseded by The Program – the New Testament. Whitlam became even more dominant in parliament in 1971, when the erratic Gorton was replaced by the clearly ludicrous Billy McMahon. The public mood became more cheerful; for better or worse, even the most rusted-on conservatives accepted that their team had finally run out of puff, and at least a couple of years – no one really thought it would be more than that – on the opposition benches were needed to regroup.

The election itself, in December 1972, was almost an anti-climax; well before polling day it was clear that the electorate had finally embraced Labor's slogan, 'It's Time', and was ready to break the habit of a lifetime and ditch the Tories in favour of – well, what? No one was quite sure, but the sense of anticipation and even relief was palpable.

My mathematical background had got me into the Whitlam bunker at Campbelltown to help with the numbers. The majority were ready to declare victory almost as soon as the count began but, remembering 1969, I insisted on waiting until at least the first figures from Western Australia – two hours behind the eastern states – came in. But very soon after I was able to declare: 'Right, we can send the white smoke up the chimney now.' Right on cue, Graham Freudenberg responded: '*Habemus Papam*.' And in a blaze of euphoria and cheap champagne, the new order was upon us.

Thus, it was a formality when Whitlam arrived at what he had long ago declared to be his destiny, and was sworn in by the governor-general, Sir Paul Hasluck, a former Liberal minister over whom he had once tossed a glass of water during a nasty exchange in parliament. But even as Hasluck, through gritted teeth, read the speech Freudenberg had written for him, announcing that the forthcoming session of parliament would seek to undo most of what he had worked for during his career in government, it seemed that he, too, had bowed to the inevitable. The hour had come at last, and so had the man.

There is a story that when the American statesman Benjamin Franklin retired from public life, he drew up plans for an impressive home in which to spend his retirement. Among other things, he informed the architect, he required a massive avenue of oak trees leading to the front door. As tactfully as possible, the architect explained that this would be difficult to arrange, as oaks took some eighty years to reach maturity. 'Then,' thundered Franklin, 'there's not a moment to lose.' Whitlam seems to have approached government in much the same mood: so much to do, so little time in which to do it.

And from his point of view, no doubt it looked relatively straightforward. As even John Howard has admitted, people knew what Whitlam stood for; he had been telling them at tiresome length, not just during the course of the campaign but for some five years before it. They really should have understood what they had voted for and what to expect. But apparently they didn't: when Whitlam had himself and his deputy, Lance Barnard, sworn in to all twenty-seven portfolios as a two-man government and began implementing The Program at breathtaking speed, a lot of people were not merely disconcerted – they were outraged.

A great many Tories had always refused to accept that Whitlam was really dedicated to Labor and its ideals; deep down, they felt, he was one of them, and on becoming prime minister would reveal himself as a sheep in wolf's clothing, unwilling to upset any apple carts or frighten any horses.

Ironically, this was also what the left of Whitlam's own party feared. But to the surprise of both sides, Whitlam turned out to be not only honest, but positively zealous.

It took the conservatives a while to get their act back together, but when they did they realised that what they were facing was a fight for the survival of the Australia they had known for the last twenty-three years: nothing less than total war would suffice. There were impressive forces at their disposal: a Senate hostile to Labor, a phalanx of ruthless and battle-hardened conservative state premiers, and a public service conditioned by a generation of Coalition rule to resist radical change.

Perhaps even more importantly, they had the inside knowledge. None of Whitlam's motley collection of twenty-seven ministers (all of whom were jumbled in together – none of this elitist nonsense about an inner cabinet) had any administrative experience. On the other side, the hard core from the Menzies years had largely dissipated, but there were any number of tough young Turks eager to show that they could play the game just as ruthlessly as their predecessors. They may only have been junior ministers but they knew their way around the bureaucracy, where they had many well-cultivated friends and allies.

And they were blessed with the certainty that a Labor government could only be a temporary aberration. After all, twenty-three years in power had shown that they alone were the natural rulers of the country. This attitude was reflected in a somewhat embarrassing sense of inadequacy and even inferiority among many of those upon whom Whitlam had so suddenly thrust power. Looking down from the press gallery, it was impossible to avoid the feeling that one was watching a match between the amateurs and the professionals, and everyone knows what the result of such a contest is likely to be.

Nonetheless, in those early days there was a huge welling of enthusiasm, not only among Labor supporters but also among the general public, who believed that indeed it had been time, and were eager to give the new boys (in those days there were no girls on the front bench) a fair go. And at least no one could say that the new government was a dull affair: for some weeks the major papers carried a regular front-page panel headed 'What the government did yesterday', which usually ran to several paragraphs.

Immediate changes ranged from the momentous (the ending of conscription and the diplomatic recognition of China) to the homely (the removal of sales tax on contraceptives in the ACT). Most of the new ministers had some pet project they were keen to push through as quickly as possible; the attorney-general, Lionel Murphy, had a formidable schedule of reform, much of which was to prove highly controversial. At the end of 1972, Whitlam read into Hansard a list of the government's major achievements to date; it took nearly half an hour. Whitlam called the list 'Apologia Pro Vita Sua'.

Despite the hectic pace, he was determined to remain at the centre of it all and took on a workload which was initially awesome, but ultimately proved to be unmanageable. The most striking feature was his insistence that he should be not only prime minister but also minister for foreign affairs; each was a full-time job under any circumstances, but under The Program they both became what would now be called 24/7 positions.

Foreign Affairs alone involved a total redrawing of relationships, not merely with individual countries but with whole continents, and at times an attempt to remap the world. One of Whitlam's first initiatives was to suggest that the boundary between Australia and the new nation of Papua New Guinea be revised to add many of the Torres Strait Islands to the latter's territory. This was put forward without consulting the inhabitants, most of whom understandably preferred to remain under the Australian welfare system; the government in Port Moresby wasn't too keen on the added responsibility either. With some regret, Whitlam withdrew the idea.

It was not the last time that his desire to tidy up maps left over from colonial times was to get him into trouble; for many years his acquiescence in the Indonesian takeover of East Timor was to cast a long shadow over his otherwise impressive record in international affairs. By then he had reluctantly handed the job over to his faithful supporter Don Willesee, but, as with other portfolios, he continued to make most of the big decisions himself.

This, of course, was one of the problems: his drive and personality tended to make the whole administration look like a one-man band. Even at the time and within the party, people referred simply to the Whitlam government – seldom if ever to the Whitlam Labor government. Even his enemies acknowledged that he was by far the best thing the party had going for it. When some of his advisers, keen to see him involved more with the general public, began by making this point, Whitlam replied wearily that he was well aware of it and would they please stop wasting his time. The days of wooing the voters were now over: the urgent task was to implement as much as possible of The Program in the weeks that were left.

This did not stop him enjoying the perks of office, the main one being overseas travel. To the dismay of the somewhat philistine press gallery who accompanied him, Whitlam preferred to spend his time stamping around art galleries and archaeological sites, rather than attending major sporting events or drinking poolside in luxury hotels, as was the prime ministerial tradition. This interest in culture got him tagged 'the tourist prime minister'; in a similar way, contributing to the welfare of war orphans in Africa was construed by his critics as giving money to overseas terrorists.

His nemesis, Malcolm Fraser, who toppled the previous opposition leader, Billy Snedden, in March 1975, successfully portrayed Whitlam's breadth of vision as an indication of hubris, a sign that he was out of touch with the everyday concerns of Australians. In a time of high and apparently intractable unemployment, of rising inflation and interest rates, there was enough truth in the accusation to start the tide running against the government. Exhilaration turned to desperation.

Some ministers resigned to grab the spoils of victory while they were still available. Others, hopelessly out of their depth and faced with a frequently hostile public service, became victims of their own incompetence. Whitlam was forced to sack two of the most senior, Jim Cairns and Rex Connor, for the crime of misleading parliament. His firmness in doing so showed a credible devotion to principle (and one which today would be seen as absurd) but added to the public impression of a government in chaos, an impression further reinforced by revelations of an attempt to borrow billions of petrodollars through channels which were at best unorthodox and at worst clandestine. There was even a pseudo-sex scandal involving Cairns' principal adviser, a woman named Junie Morosi.

It did not help that Whitlam, while personally behaving impeccably as things went from bad to worse to impossible, remained preoccupied with the big picture. By the time a drastic ministerial reshuffle and a final hardline budget started to get things back on the rails, it was far too late; the government was clearly doomed. But Fraser couldn't wait: he blocked supply and the governor-general, Sir John Kerr, dismissed the government, forcing an election in which Whitlam, for all his bravado, never had a hope. He clung to the leadership for two more years until another crushing electoral defeat compelled him to resign.

But his dismissal had an unexpected consequence. He would always have been remembered as the finest parliamentarian of his era, the man who brought the Labor Party back from twenty-three years in the wilderness, whose great, if ultimately flawed, program changed the structure of Australia and inspired a generation with a renewed belief in the possibility of rational, visionary reform within the parliamentary system. But Fraser and Kerr made him more than that: a political martyr, a heroic and tragic figure of Shakespearean proportions.

The left, which had once doubted him, now embraced him as a secular saint. Even his failures and misjudgements – it was revealed that as well as the disastrous miscalculation of the petrodollars affair, Whitlam had been involved in a plan to restore Labor's finances with a loan from the Iraqi Ba'ath Party – failed to crack the image. Whitlam himself thrived on it, taking the job of Australia's ambassador to UNESCO and later making public appearances in roles ranging from chairman of the National Gallery to spruiker for a brand of spaghetti sauce. He became a fixture at opening nights and political funerals. It should have been faintly bathetic, but instead every appearance seemed to increase his stature and his place in public affection. Whenever lists were drawn up of Australia's living national treasures, the name of Edward Gough Whitlam was invariably towards the top.

In part, the regard was nostalgic: a yearning for times when politics was more open and positive, when it did not always seem to be a contest between greed and fear, when vision was still considered a desirable thing in a prime minister and when 'do-gooder' was not an insult. But more than that, it was a recognition not just of achievement, but of style. The Whitlam government undoubtedly had its downside, but it was always pushing the barriers; it was a government of panache and pizzazz.

Whitlam once told an illustrious gathering that his preferred sport was rowing: 'It is, of course, an extraordinarily apt sport for men in public life because you can face one way while going the other.' A good line, but it could never be applied to the man himself. Whitlam was always going forward, and his eyes were always fixed on the stars.

LANCE BARNARD

SOME POLITICIANS ARE BORN TO LEAD, OTHERS TO FOLLOW. Lance Barnard was one of the latter, but he was the kind of follower every leader dreams of.

Unfailingly loyal, an enthusiastic collaborator in the good times and a stalwart ally in the bad ones, he stood by Gough Whitlam's side for twenty years – twenty of the most tumultuous years in Australia's political history. And when he went, his departure was the signal for the fall, not only of his leader, but of the Labor Party as we knew it. He was only ever a number two, a deputy and a deliberately unobtrusive one at that. But he had more influence than many of those who occupied the Lodge.

In a sense, he was born to the role. In northern Tasmania, and in Launceston in particular, the Barnards were not merely an institution; they formed something of a political dynasty. Lance's father, Claude, a railway man, was the long-serving Labor member for the federal seat of Bass and a minister in the postwar government of Ben Chifley; he lost the seat in

1949 but moved seamlessly to the state House of Assembly, in which he remained until his death in 1957. In the meantime, Lance had regained Bass in the 1954 election and retained it until his retirement in 1975. By then, he had become irreplaceable. Labor has struggled to hold the seat ever since.

Lance Herbert Barnard may have inherited the seat, but he brought to it impeccable credentials of his own. He had served in the 9th Division at El Alamein, and in civilian life had become a highly respected schoolteacher. But there was never any doubt that politics would be his vocation. Coincidentally, he arrived in Canberra just one year after Gough Whitlam, and the two men struck up an immediate friendship that became one of the great political bonds of recent times. In his eulogy at Barnard's funeral in 1997, Whitlam noted that Barnard was the first of his colleagues to suggest that Whitlam should run for a leadership role: in 1959 he had urged Whitlam to nominate for the position of deputy, which was likely to become vacant in the near future. Not that Whitlam needed any encouragement – but it was reassuring to find his own self-assessment confirmed by a more earthy and practical judge.

Barnard quickly became a figure of consequence in his own right; his colleagues recognised his integrity, and his ability to contain conflict and resolve disputes within the caucus and beyond. When Whitlam became leader of the party in 1967, Barnard was elected unopposed as his deputy, and the pair immediately set about the great task of party reform. Whitlam, of course, was the passionate one, the zealot; Barnard undertook the less glamorous but equally essential spade-work, all the while watching his leader's back.

The importance of this became apparent in 1968, when Whitlam, exasperated at the lack of progress, put his leadership on the line in the first of his celebrated 'crash through or crash' ultimatums. He was challenged by the Left's popular and charismatic Jim Cairns, who had his own share of enemies in the party room. Moderates urged Barnard to run as a consensus candidate, and had he done so he would almost certainly have won the leadership. But he stayed loyal; by this stage he had become convinced that Whitlam was Labor's best and perhaps only hope of winning back government. His support ensured Whitlam's victory in what was an uncomfortably close result. From then on, the pair surged towards the final victory of 1972.

I first met Barnard through his press secretary, Clem Lloyd, who was everything Barnard was not. A huge, rambunctious journalist, fond of the pub and the punt, Lloyd's permanently dishevelled exterior housed one the best political brains in Canberra. He had made Barnard's office a meeting and drinking place for like-minded souls from the press gallery, and I quickly drifted into the group. Barnard, on his infrequent appearances, seemed resigned to the situation and somewhat amused by it; he knew Lloyd's value and trusted him to look after his interests, which Lloyd invariably did. The deputy leader was a nuggety, medium-sized man with an open and cheerful Irish face, clad in a sober grey suit and sporting a rather dated grey hat, which he frequently forgot to remove indoors.

It was immediately clear why he was so well liked in a profession notorious for its suspicions and animosities: Lance Barnard was a man without guile, absolutely straight, the type my parents used to call the salt of the earth. After even a brief chat, I appreciated the strength and depth of his commitment to the Labor cause, and to Whitlam's crusade to modernise the party structure and to make the party electable. To Barnard, this had nothing to do with ideology or the rivalries of the state machines or the ambitions of the warlords involved; it was simply a matter of common sense. His down-to-earth approach made him the perfect foil to Whitlam's visionary ambitions.

But it also made him close to invisible. His more extroverted colleagues – Jim Cairns, Lionel Murphy, Clyde Cameron, Tom Uren, even Al Grassby – were constantly in the news, yet Barnard remained an obscure, almost anonymous, figure. But, as a surprised public realised after the 1972 'It's Time' election installed him as deputy prime minister, he was to be one of the movers and shakers in the seismic changes that followed.

For starters, Whitlam formed his duumvirate, unwilling to wait for the final election results to be declared or for caucus to meet to elect a new ministry. He boasted to parliament: 'The first Whitlam ministry was the smallest ministry with jurisdiction over Australia since the Duke of Wellington formed a ministry with two other ministers 138 years previously.' Barnard actually had the lion's share of it – fourteen departments to Whitlam's thirteen. And the first headline-making decision was his: to end national service and free all the conscripts currently in camps. It was a groundbreaking indication of the storm of changes to come, and the more ironic because, as Whitlam also pointed out, the duumvirate was the first ministry composed entirely of returned servicemen.

When the normal system was reinstated, Barnard was sworn in as minister for defence and given the herculean task of unifying the five rival departments of army, navy, air force, supply and repatriation. He did a pretty good job of it, but it is fair to say that many if not all of his successors have cursed him for the move as they struggled to master the resulting behemoth that is the combined defence department.

Barnard's life was not made any easier by the fact that the head of the new department was the formidable Sir Arthur Tange, also known as Sir After Dark due to his unrivalled capacity for manoeuvring and conspiring to produce the outcomes he wanted. Few of these coincided with the aims of the new government. Tange was the last and toughest of the Cold War warriors in the public service; many in the Labor Party felt that his commitment to the anti-communist Western Alliance overrode any loyalty he might feel towards his elected government. Certainly it was known that he had been appalled when, immediately after the election, a series of senior Labor figures publicly criticised the US president, Richard Nixon, for resuming the bombing of Hanoi in a last-ditch attempt to turn the war around.

Barnard had not been among them, but Tange still viewed the arrival of the Labor government as a dangerous aberration, to be brought as far under control as was possible. Barnard himself, as the elected deputy head of government, was invulnerable, but the same did not apply to his staff. Tange informed his new minister that his confidante Clem Lloyd and another senior adviser, Brian Toohey, were not to attend secret defence briefings; the implication was that they were security risks. Barnard reluctantly accepted this bureaucratic verdict: Lloyd and Toohey, furious and humiliated, resigned on the spot, leaving gaps that could never be filled. Their replacements were well-meaning and competent, but they lacked the long experience and deep political instinct that had given Barnard's office its clout within the Labor Party.

As a result, after the 1974 election Barnard lost the deputy leadership to the more popular, and more erratic, Jim Cairns. He struggled on in his mammoth and unwieldy portfolio and continued to produce results, but his days of power and influence were over, and in 1975, exhausted and somewhat disillusioned, he resigned.

Barnard claimed a reward for his years of loyal service: he asked Whitlam for an ambassadorship to the Scandinavian bloc of Sweden, Norway and Finland. The party apparatchiks were horrified; by this time the government was in serious trouble, and to have one of its most senior figures abandon the struggle for a rich and comfortable sinecure was the worst possible look. There were muttered references to rats and sinking ships. The party president, Bob Hawke, described it as 'an act of political lunacy' and the party secretary, David Combe, warned: 'We look like a party of junketeers who do not expect to be in office often or long.'

But Whitlam would deny his old friend nothing. Indeed, he had even sounded Barnard out about succeeding Sir Paul Hasluck as governor-general, but Barnard, more aware of his Labor roots than his colleague Bill Hayden later proved to be, declined the offer. He left Canberra under something of a cloud, and the consequences were immediate and severe. The Barnard family had made the seat of Bass their personal fiefdom; there was now a vacuum that the party was unable to fill. The by-election candidate, another schoolteacher named John Macrostie, was, to put it mildly, inadequate. Despite Whitlam's vigorous personal campaign, the Liberals won the seat comfortably. The loss was seen as a forerunner to the electoral landslide waiting to engulf Labor at the general election.

Barnard returned to Australia in 1978, and in 1981 Malcolm Fraser made him director of the Office of Australian War Graves, an appointment which showed the bipartisan regard in which he was still held. He retired two years later and died in 1997. Whitlam gave a heartfelt eulogy in which he described Barnard as having been the Ben Chifley to his own John Curtin, one of the great political partnerships. But for Whitlam it was more than that: in a career in which alliances frequently shifted, in which Whitlam had made more enemies than friends, Barnard had been the rock on which he could always rely. He was, Whitlam proclaimed, 'my oldest and best mate'.

LIONEL MURPHY

F GOUGH WHITLAM WAS THE PUBLIC FACE OF HIS SHORT-LIVED government and Jim Cairns the heart it wore on its sleeve, then Lionel Murphy was surely the brains in the backroom. More than anyone else, Murphy was responsible for planning and implementing the program of social and legal reform that took place between 1972 and 1975; and therefore more than anyone else he was demonised and pursued by the establishment into and beyond his premature grave. Even today there are people in the clubs of Sydney and Melbourne who can hardly bear to mention his name without making ritual motions of exorcism.

But if he was an object of fear and loathing on the right, he was admired, venerated and even loved by the left. As with the hate, the love endured beyond his death. When Murphy died in 1986, Michael Kirby, by then, like Murphy, a judge of the High Court, recalled:

He died, as he had lived, in the midst of controversy.

But then an amazing thing happened. An unprecedented and secular demonstration of the man and his
life took place in the Sydney Town Hall. Thousands of
his fellow citizens walked silently and with reverence
into that great civic arena. I have never before seen such
an assembly of Australian leaders. The governor-
general and the governor, the prime minister and most
of the cabinet, leading members of the opposition,
every remaining justice of the High Court, most of the
judges of appeal and many Supreme Court judges,
heads of departments, scientists, schoolchildren and
citizens … What were these Australian citizens – most
of whom were there out of love and not duty – trying to
say about this unusual man?

What indeed? Perhaps it was no more than an acknowledgement that even if Murphy had not always been liked, appreciated or understood, he was never a man who could be ignored.

His complexity baffled even those close to him. The journalist David Halpin, who worked as his press secretary during
the last of his opposition years, summed him up thus:

> On the surface Lionel was gregarious, affable (when
> not tired or affected by Johnnie Walker), willing to
> listen to media advice, ambitious, attuned to the then
> faint stirrings of feminism and sinuously charming.
> Underneath he could be manipulative, vain, thought-
> less, blind to advice about why journalists were culti-
> vating him, disturbingly envious of Gough's position,

34

a willing believer in conspiracy theories and ruthless
in the pursuit of self-interest.

And, Halpin could have added, driven by intellectual curiosity, reformist zeal and political ambition – not always in the same direction. When focused, Murphy was formidable, unstoppable. But much of his life was spent, in the splendid phrase of humourist Stephen Leacock, riding madly off in all directions.

He held degrees in both law and science, an unusual combination which held its own contradictions. Murphy the scientist was rational, analytic, capable of brushing aside the bullshit to arrive at the only sensible conclusion. But the law is not always rational; winning a case often involves the copious application of bullshit to disguise its inherent weakness. Of course, the same applies to politics.

Murphy was openly contemptuous of this aspect of his chosen career, but it fascinated him nonetheless and on occasion he could be very good at it. As an advocate, whether in the courtroom or the Senate, he had few peers. The problem was that he was easily swept away by new thoughts and fresh ideas. It was not unusual for Murphy to espouse opposite sides of the same argument, with equal passion and sincerity, within the course of a week. It made his brand of politics both exhilarating and confusing.

It also meant that, despite the contrary belief of himself and his supporters, he was too erratic for true leadership. But this never prevented him from seeking it. His relationship with Whitlam was always one of rivalry, and seldom friendly or even cordial. Murphy opted to stand for the Senate rather than the House of Representatives because it offered a quicker and easier path towards the top, although not all the way. When he decided he was more suited than Whitlam to lead the party he tried half-heartedly to make the switch, but was denied. He then settled back to make the most of the not-inconsiderable power he already had, and to appropriate the role of a kind of de facto leader both within the party and the parliament.

For three glorious years he was spectacularly successful. In 1967 Whitlam had been elected leader of the party, but the Left – of which Murphy was the senior parliamentary representative, if not actually the titular head – still ran the party machine. It was not until the transmogrification of the Victorian branch at the end of 1970 that that balance finally changed. When Whitlam and his ally, federal secretary Cyril Wyndham, finally persuaded the party that the parliamentary leadership should be entitled to seats on the federal executive, the party's day-to-day governing body, the Left insisted that this should apply not only to the leaders in the Reps but also to those in the Senate. This ensured that the votes of Murphy and his deputy, Sam Cohen, would regularly cancel out those of Whitlam and his deputy, Lance Barnard. Within the party hierarchy, Murphy was at least the equal of his nominal leader.

In Canberra he was a good deal stronger. Murphy devoted himself to building up the role of the Senate, traditionally the target of abolition by Labor – and especially by the Left. At the time neither the conservative government nor the Labor opposition held a majority in the upper house; the

balance of power was in the hands of the breakaway Democratic Labor Party, regarded as rats and traitors by all right-
thinking ALP members. But Murphy was always willing to
deal with them, stroking and cajoling them into supporting
him when he saw an advantage.

At the same time, he developed the fledgling Senate committee system into a highly effective inquisitorial force which
could be, and was, frequently used to embarrass the government. Colleagues warned Murphy at the time that he was creating a monster that would one day be used against Labor, but
he was more interested in the short-term gains he was making. Years later, he did not appreciate the irony when the full
force of his brainchild was turned to his own destruction.

Those final years of opposition were probably the high
point of Murphy's political power and influence. Although he
finally lost the battle over state aid, he was one of the key policy makers leading up to 1972. The legal and constitutional
platform which underpinned the whole of Labor's reform
program was largely his work, as were the commitments to
consumer protection and no-fault divorce. His leadership in
the Senate and the headaches it caused the government had a
lot to do with the destabilisation of Harold Holt, John Gorton
and William McMahon, and with the creation of the 'It's
Time' mood which brought Labor back to power. Labor could
have won without Murphy, but it would have been harder and
it would have formed a very different sort of government.

Murphy flung himself into the role of attorney-general with
almost manic enthusiasm. While the whole ministry was setting a blistering pace, Murphy's energy remains outstanding.

In just over two years he transformed the legal landscape. Among his more obvious achievements were the *Family Law Act*, the *Trade Practices Act*, the Prices Justification Tribunal, the Law Reform Commission, the *Companies Act*, the Administrative Appeals Tribunal, the abolition of capital punishment, freedom of information legislation, Aboriginal land rights, Legal Aid, the federal ombudsman, the Federal Court, censorship reform, endangered species legislation and plans for the Securities and Exchange Commission. He also lifted the restrictions on home brewing. In his spare time he ran Australia's case against French nuclear testing in the World Court at The Hague, guided his own and his colleagues' hectic legislative program through the Senate, and ran the rapidly growing attorney-general's department. Graham Freudenberg later claimed that Murphy's record of reform as attorney-general was unmatched since the days of Alfred Deakin.

Unfortunately, the record didn't end there. Murphy's passion for politics remained undimmed, but his skills seemed to desert him. His raid on ASIO's headquarters in Melbourne in March 1973 has gone into legend as one of the great authoritarian blunders in Australian history. It wasn't; any element of police stateism about it was dissipated by the sight of a somewhat hungover Murphy facing a bank of television cameras in the bleak Melbourne dawn, and complaining to his then press secretary, George Negus: 'Jesus, George, what have you done to me?' It was more farcical than sinister. But it abruptly ended whatever honeymoon the new government might have enjoyed with the electorate, and Murphy, like his acolyte and successor Gareth Evans many years later, gained a reputation for being accident-prone.

It was a reputation compounded by his part in the so-called Gair affair, which led to the 1974 election. The government had hatched a plan to gain control of the Senate by appointing a DLP senator from Queensland, Vince Gair, to a diplomatic post. There was a half-Senate election due later in the year; if Gair left, there would be six, rather than five, Senate seats up for grabs, and Labor stood a good chance of winning the sixth. Murphy immersed himself in the conspiracy, but neither he nor anyone else paid attention to the finer constitutional detail, and Australia was treated to the spectacle of the government's finest legal mind being effortlessly outmanoeuvred by Queensland's peanut-farmer premier, Joh Bjelke-Petersen: after getting wind of the plot, Bjelke-Petersen had the Queensland state governor issue the election writs before Gair had formally resigned, foiling the government's plans. When the error was revealed, Whitlam roared at his staff: 'Get me Murphy.' Rather unfairly, the attorney-general was made to carry the can.

He also took more than his fair share of the blame for not foreseeing the disastrous consequences of the loans affair several months later. The attempt to borrow vast sums of loose petrodollars through unorthodox sources (that is, shysters wearing cream sneakers and green sunglasses) was always likely to come unstuck, and anyone with a modicum of common sense should have realised it – Murphy's standing as the country's first legal officer seemed an unnecessary qualification.

In the circumstances, Whitlam needed little persuading when an opportunity arose to fill a vacancy on the High Court early in 1975. Murphy was elevated with almost indecent haste. Bill Hayden later told the story of how the ultra-conservative chief justice, Sir Garfield Barwick, harangued him vigorously about what a mess the appointment had made of the High Court. When Hayden told Whitlam, Whitlam replied: 'Yes, but did you tell him how much we'd improved cabinet?'

Murphy was indeed an unlikely and often lonely figure on the bench. He refused to indulge in the pomp and ceremony that so delighted Barwick and sat without a wig or a gown. His brother judges mainly subscribed to a literal and legalistic interpretation of their role, and Murphy generally found himself in a minority – frequently a minority of one. Today, many of his judgements are greatly admired for their breadth of vision and their ability to link the law to the rest of society; one in particular, which included the memorable sentence 'Mr Neal is entitled to be an agitator', inspired a television documentary. Murphy would have found himself more at home in the High Court that produced the *Mabo* decision, revoking the fiction of *terra nullius*, and which discovered an implied right of free speech in the constitution. But the narrow, black-letter law approach which made the Barwick court so admired by the architects of tax avoidance schemes was constricting, especially as Barwick did his best to keep Murphy away from the more controversial cases.

There were also complaints from the establishment, at first sporadic but later more orchestrated, that his social behaviour was unsuited to his position. Murphy, like Bob Hawke and John Gorton, whose conduct he vigorously defended, was something of a womaniser; his pre-marital success rate was a source of wonder and envy to his colleagues, who could not understand how a man once described in a pro-mining pamphlet as 'the puce-nosed jackal' could get for free so much of what many of them had to rent, in David Halpin's neat phrase.

Again like Hawke and Gorton, he also liked a drink. In his opposition days he and Sir John Kerr, after a very long lunch, were once noticed attempting to negotiate the Parliament House steps, at the bottom of which a Commonwealth car was waiting patiently. A considerate reporter helped them in their descent and waited to be thanked. Murphy looked at him wearily. 'You stupid bastard,' he said. 'We were going up the steps, not down them.'

As a judge, Murphy curbed both these habits. But what infuriated the conservatives was his refusal to give up his old friends. Murphy was no Prince Hal. 'Why should I change?' he said to Clyde Cameron, adding that none of his fellow judges had done so. 'They still visit the Melbourne Club and associate with their conservative and reactionary friends. Why shouldn't I visit the places I used to frequent before my appointment and continue to associate with my Labor friends?'

To Murphy the rationalist it was logical enough, but Murphy the politician should have seen that it wouldn't wash. To the establishment and to the media, there was a world of difference between a judge dropping a few quiet hints on tax evasion to a business acquaintance over the billiard table, and

Murphy making enquiries on behalf of his 'little mate', a Sydney solicitor named Morgan Ryan who was facing charges of forgery and conspiracy. In 1984 the *Age* published illegal tape recordings revealing the latter conversation; the hunt for Murphy was on, and it was unrelenting. His enemies pursued him through the Senate by means of the committees he had personally empowered, and eventually through the courts. He was acquitted once, but this only made the hunters more determined. Only his terminal cancer curtailed the chase, and even then one conservative politician declared that he would not be satisfied until he had seen Murphy buried at a crossroads with a stake through his heart.

His friends and supporters claimed him as a martyr. Clyde Cameron called him 'a great lawyer, a great judge, a great radical and a great Laborite'. More recently, his rehabilitation, as both a reformer and a judge, has begun. Books and articles are starting to appear which at least attempt to separate the man from his achievements, and to consider the latter dispassionately. But it is hard to do: his work and life were too much part of each other. His zest for ideas, his hatred of hypocrisy and his contempt for privilege coloured everything he said, everything he did, everything he was. You could agree or disagree, love him or hate him. But Murphy was never a man you could ignore or forget.

JIM CAIRNS

T SEEMS HARD TO BELIEVE NOW, BUT FOR SOME YEARS
Jim Cairns was thought of as a genuine leadership rival to
Gough Whitlam – the true-blue Labor man of the Left,
the guardian of the party's great traditions, as opposed to
the brash, domineering lawyer who wanted to take the ALP
by the scruff of the neck and drag it into modern times,
whether it wished to come or not.

Thus, when Cairns challenged Whitlam under the slogan
'Whose party is it – his or ours?' as late as 1968, it resonated,
and the contest turned out to be far closer than anyone had
predicted. In the end the two men were reconciled – well, sort
of – and Cairns' tragic fall from politics prefigured Whitlam's
far more spectacular and memorable one. Even forty years on,
it is hard to think of one man without recalling the other.

Few Australian politicians have evoked more passion
than Cairns, and few have been harder to evaluate. The high
points of his extraordinary life – his leadership of the anti-
war movement and his rise to the deputy prime ministership –

were matched by some equally spectacular lows: he was the only treasurer never to deliver a budget, and was eventually sacked from the ministry for misleading parliament. He went from being a hero of the left, both inside and outside parliament, to becoming a political outcast whose eccentricities were tolerated only because of the triumphs of the past.

His most loyal and longstanding mate, Tom Uren, once described Cairns as the most Christ-like man he had ever known, yet even Uren was forced to admit that Cairns was not really suited to politics. In the end, Cairns accepted that himself.

He was an only and lonely child who never knew his father. Raised by his mother and grandmother, he learnt self-control and self-sufficiency at an early age. He was a proficient sportsman, excelling in the most difficult of disciplines, the decathlon. Like Bill Hayden, he joined the police force but found few of his fellow officers shared his idealism. He resumed his studies and gained a commerce degree, and later a doctorate, from the University of Melbourne.

He entered parliament in 1955, and immediately became a leading figure on the left and a student of foreign policy, especially in Indo-China. Cairns would later be accused of taking a naive approach to the war in Vietnam, but in fact he was well ahead of his critics. Long before Australia became involved in the conflict, Cairns had pointed out the fallacy of considering the complicated strands of Asian communism and nationalism as some kind of monolithic force bent on world domination.

Although Cairns had little in common with his leader and fellow Victorian Arthur Calwell, the two were united in a dislike and distrust of Gough Whitlam, who was clearly grooming himself as Calwell's successor. Calwell backed Cairns against Whitlam, but when Calwell was finally forced to retire after Labor's devastating loss in the 1966 election, Cairns could not even beat Lance Barnard for the deputy's job. To add to his setbacks, Calwell refused to vacate the safe seat of Melbourne for Cairns after Cairns' own seat of Yarra was abolished in a redistribution.

He had his best chance in April 1968, when Whitlam dramatically resigned the leadership in an attempt to force a showdown with the ALP federal executive, and in particular the Victorian delegates, who backed Cairns. Cairns lost the ballot narrowly, 32 to 38, giving Whitlam and his supporters a terrible fright.

In the meantime, Cairns' popular support was growing steadily as opposition to the war in Vietnam mounted. In 1970 it reached an all-time high when Cairns led a protest of over 70,000 people through the streets of Melbourne. His enemies said he was more interested in being king of the kids than in his duties as a member of parliament, and he did nothing to correct this impression; in one of his numerous speeches at universities, he said, 'I sincerely hope that authority has had its day.' But there can be no doubt that the protest movement he headed contributed significantly to the 'It's Time' mood which finally brought Labor to power in 1972.

Once in government, Cairns immediately showed that he was not going to change, joining Uren and Clyde Cameron in publicly condemning Nixon for the Christmas bombing of Hanoi. This began a period of tension between Washington and Canberra, which was greatly exacerbated when Cairns became deputy prime minister after the 1974 election. In August that year he somewhat reluctantly replaced Frank Crean as treasurer, having been pushed to take the job by his leftist colleagues.

He enjoyed a period as acting prime minister while Whitlam was overseas at the start of 1975, but although few people realised it, his political career was already in decline. Cairns was going through a period of self-doubt and disillusionment with the formal political process. To his friends he spoke of the need for love and cooperation to replace confrontation. In one speech on the economy he stated: 'What is needed is not just a way to control inflation but a way to reform society so that it may avoid inflation.' The hardheads at Treasury were not impressed.

On 2 December 1974, Cairns appointed Junie Morosi, a Filipina mother of three, as his office coordinator. It rapidly became clear that she had an extraordinary influence over him. Caucus colleagues, Treasury officials and even fellow ministers were barred from entry to his office. In their place came a number of anonymous businessmen, friends and acquaintances (it turned out) of Morosi's husband, David Ditchburn. Old allies like Uren urged Cairns to fire Morosi, but he refused to listen. At Labor's national conference at Terrigal in 1975, Cairns made headlines by confessing to 'a kind of love' for Morosi, but by then it was obvious to all that it was a lot more than that. After a life in which most of his considerable passion had been diverted to political causes, Cairns had finally fallen like a ton of bricks.

His office soon became completely unworkable, and Whitlam moved him into the junior environment portfolio before he could deliver his first budget. Shortly afterwards he was found to have signed a letter authorising George Harris, a Melbourne businessman, to raise loans on the government's behalf. Because Cairns had categorically denied doing so to parliament, Whitlam sacked him for misleading the house. He served one term in opposition and retired at the end of 1977.

To the surprise of many, Morosi stuck with him. They organised a new-age festival of love and peace on some land outside Canberra, which was to be bought with the proceeds to set up a commune; when Morosi's relatives later chased some hippy squatters off at gunpoint, Cairns refused to intervene. The pair ran an ice-cream shop at nearby Bungendore for some time; eventually Cairns returned to his farm near Melbourne, where he wrote books and sold them personally at the Prahran market. These were his last public appearances.

Politically, he remains an enigma. He was a huge influence in the late '60s and early '70s in opposition, but by and large a failure in government. Perhaps he summed it up best himself after his dismissal. 'I wear my heart too easily on my sleeve,' he said in a rare personal moment. It is a luxury politicians cannot afford, but it was the mark of a man whose courage and conviction were never in doubt.

CLYDE CAMERON

LYDE ROBERT CAMERON SET ONE POLITICAL RECORD THAT is unlikely to be broken – not that anyone would want to break it. He sat in the House of Representatives for a total of thirty-one years, and twenty-eight of them were spent on the opposition benches.

He lived through two World Wars, as well as Australian deployments in Korea, Malaya and Vietnam, and survived three Labor Party splits – four, if you count Joe Lyons' defection to become a Nationalist prime minister. It is hardly surprising that Cameron earned a reputation as a bitter and vindictive politician. What is more remarkable is that he had a brief, positive renaissance under Gough Whitlam, during which he realised many of his long-term ambitions, before, once again, it all ended in acrimony.

For about five years, from 1969 until 1975, the two men travelled in lockstep, the firmest of allies – so much so that after the 1972 election, Whitlam gave his colleague a photograph inscribed, with genuine gratitude, 'To Clyde, a principal architect of victory.' During this period the two men made one of the oddest political couples ever seen even within the ALP, always a party of strange and unlikely coalitions.

Whitlam, the urbane Sydney lawyer, a natural politician of the Right, classically educated and well connected, always prepared to negotiate a path through whatever obstacles stood between himself and political victory; a man of high intellect and high ideals, but one who always acknowledged the need for pragmatism.

Compare and contrast, as Whitlam himself often put it, Cameron, a lifelong lefty who had left school at fifteen to go shearing, whose politics were forged in bitter and uncompromising disputes within the Australian Workers' Union, who never forgave his enemies and saw every contest as a personal challenge to be won by any means available, irrespective of legality or ethics.

What drew him to Whitlam was the shining possibility of finally achieving office. Cameron had entered parliament in 1949, the year Labor lost office. After the death of his beloved Ben Chifley, he had remained loyal to Bert ('the Doc') Evatt, only to see him lose three successive elections. Then Arthur Calwell lost another three.

A fierce, stocky figure, Cameron, now white-haired and myopic behind heavy spectacles, grew ever more frustrated and even desperate. Bill Wentworth, a constant opponent of Cameron in parliament during this period, described him as a fearsome and predatory owl. He gave endless speeches inside and outside parliament on injustice in all its forms, often passionate and erudite but always, in the end, impotent.

Cameron's generation of Labor men seemed doomed to perpetual opposition until, more or less coinciding with the retirement of the invincible Bob Menzies, Whitlam began what was to prove his irresistible rise. In every sense – class, ideology, political backers – Whitlam was Cameron's natural enemy. But he offered the only hope of Cameron achieving his dream: to become minister for labour.

At the beginning of 1969, Whitlam put it to him as a stark choice: if he joined the bandwagon for reform of the party structure, which was needed to persuade the voters that Labor was electable, he could have his heart's desire. The alternative was to grow old in opposition. Cameron went for the gold.

As a member of the party's all-powerful federal executive, he was a powerbroker whose influence extended far beyond his home state of South Australia. In the past he had invariably voted with the Left majority, based in Victoria with support from Queensland and Western Australia. Now he and his fellow South Australian delegate Mick Young, shortly to become federal secretary, switched to back Whitlam on the crucial issue of providing state aid for all schools, private as well as public, on a needs basis.

This change, combined with Whitlam's charisma and the Gorton government's blunderings, was by itself nearly enough to win the subsequent federal election, but Victoria, still under the control of the hard Left, failed to follow the national trend and delivered only one seat. Whitlam decided the branch must be rebuilt, and asked for Cameron's help. After some agonising, Cameron agreed – on condition that the right-wing New South Wales branch should suffer the same fate. And so the deal was done.

When the ambush was sprung at the next executive meeting in Broken Hill, the New South Wales delegates, pre-warned, accepted federal intervention. The Victorians, realising they had been trapped, fought back. One delegate, Bill Brown, thunderously and almost tearfully denounced the treachery of his traditional allies, including Cameron. The latter, momentarily abashed, took a backward step; rather than an intervention, he said, he would settle for an inquiry.

Brown triumphantly went off to ring Melbourne with the good news, but inadvertently left the door of his room open; Cameron, passing by, heard every word of his boasts about how he had out-bluffed the silly old bugger. From then on, an inquiry was off the agenda; so was mere intervention. The sentence now was execution.

In the weeks that followed, Cameron joined the Victorian reform group in gathering evidence against the ruling clique; during this period, Whitlam (LLB, QC) described himself as Cameron's junior. His union years had taught Cameron a lot about the law; indeed, Bob Hawke and others described him as one of the best untrained legal brains they had ever struck. Cameron, exhibiting no false modesty, enthusiastically agreed.

Certainly his diligence paid off. At its next meeting in Melbourne, the ALP federal executive voted formally to abolish its Victorian branch and remake it in a more voter-friendly fashion. This was the last real hurdle before the 1972 election.

At the final rising of the parliament, it is traditional for members to make sentimental speeches about how much they really like each other and how they will miss their departing colleagues; in 1972, Cameron's contribution was anything but sentimental. True to form, he paid out a few old enemies and gave the Coalition government a thorough tongue-lashing: its overthrow was long overdue, and he felt only pleasure in predicting many of its members would lose their seats.

In the event, it wasn't quite as many as he had hoped – but when the parliament sat again in 1973, Cameron was sitting on the right of the speaker, having been sworn in as minister for labour; in the reshuffle after the 1974 double dissolution, he was to add immigration to his portfolio.

Whitlam imposed just one condition: Cameron was not to use his ministerial position to pursue his feud within the AWU against its leader, Tom Dougherty. As it happened, Dougherty died in office a few weeks before Labor won government, rather to Cameron's disappointment; he had hoped to see Dougherty dumped by the membership.

When Bob Hawke, as president of the ACTU, attended Dougherty's funeral, Cameron blasted him: 'What you have done is to pay your last respects to the most evil man ever to hold office in any trade union. You presided over the funeral of a cruel, arrogant, deceitful, hypocritical, malevolent, treacherous and lecherous man. One of the worst criminals ever to escape the gallows, a gangster, a thief, a thug, a blackmailer, a ballot rigger, a wife starver, a traitor to his union, a standover man, a giver and taker of bribes, a tyrant and a coward.' Cameron was seldom afraid to say what he thought.

As minister, he decided to treat the public service as a kind of testing ground for the rest of the workforce. He introduced equal pay and the concept of flexitime, allowing workers to stagger their hours, principally to accommodate school-age children. The latter was immediately turned into a rort whereby large numbers wangled extra days off on the ski-fields of Thredbo or the beaches of the South Coast. In response, Cameron attacked the fat cats – senior public-service executives whom he believed were the main abusers of the system.

Such public controversies overshadowed much of the genuine reform he brought to the industrial scene; for instance, his appointment of the maverick barrister Jim Staples to the bench of the Industrial Commission received far more attention than the appointments of Elizabeth Evatt, Mary Gaudron and Michael Kirby, all of whom he launched on their judicial careers.

But as the inflation resulting from the international oil-price shocks started to envelop the government, Cameron was as bereft of remedies as every other minister. In one celebrated exchange in cabinet, Whitlam rounded on him. 'What would a fucking ex-shearer know about economics?' the prime minister shouted. 'Well,' replied Cameron calmly, 'at least as much as a fucking ex-scholar of classical Greek.'

But the real falling-out came when Whitlam, his government well and truly on the skids as the various scandals of 1975 gathered momentum, performed his last, fateful reshuffle. In an attempt to give the ministry a new look, he relegated

Cameron to the junior ministry of science and consumer affairs and gave his beloved ministry of labour to a blow-in Sydney lawyer, 'Diamond' Jim McClelland. At first Cameron simply refused to leave his office; even after Whitlam himself blundered through the staff area and into Cameron's office, he stayed put.

Eventually a delegation of left-wing colleagues, led by Tom Uren and Moss Cass, persuaded Cameron to accept the inevitable. His only memorable performance in his new and despised job was to hold a long and public argument with Whitlam over the pronunciation of the word 'kilogram' – interestingly, on this one the shearer was right and the Greek scholar wrong.

After the wipeout of 1975, Cameron spent much of his time plotting, unsuccessfully, to have Whitlam replaced as leader, first by Lionel Bowen and then by Bill Hayden. Whitlam resigned in favour of Hayden after the 1977 election, but when Bob Hawke arrived in parliament in 1980 Cameron shifted his support again.

By this time he had retired from active politics, although he kept in touch and in fact conducted lengthy interviews for the National Library's oral history program, with, among others, Garfield Barwick; if that is ever released it will make interesting reading. He also published a couple of books of his own, although most of the extensive diaries he kept while in office were mysteriously stolen.

But he never forgave Whitlam. Some years later, Barry Cohen, then a minister in the Hawke government, took a trip to China during which he got into a discussion with a Chinese apparatchik over the merits of their different forms of government. Having put the view that the Chinese hierarchy was less than democratic, Cohen was surprised at the spirited reply: in comparison, Australia was positively dictatorial. Why, there the leader could sack his ministers for no reason, against the will of the people, on a personal whim, an act of petty spite … After a bit more of this, the penny dropped. 'Have you,' asked Cohen, 'by any chance been talking to a Mr Clyde Cameron?' Well, yes. To the last, Cameron relished his vendettas.

BILL HAYDEN

N THE IMMEDIATE AFTERMATH OF LABOR'S WIN IN 1972, ALL the attention was on the duumvirate of Gough Whitlam and Lance Barnard as they tore into the accumulated detritus of twenty-three years of conservative rule. The dynamic duo left very little room in the headlines for anyone else. But on the whole, even those who had been most vocal in opposition were prepared to bide their time and brood on the magnitude of the task ahead of them.

One such was Bill Hayden, who, as minister for social security, would have the job of implementing what was to become Labor's most important and long-lasting reform: the national healthcare scheme designed by Dick Scotton and John Deeble. Along with the end of conscription and the institution of free universities, this was perhaps the most anticipated of the reforms flagged by Whitlam for nearly four years, but it was still bitterly contested by the conservative medical profession and their allies in the Coalition. It would obviously be a vital and bitterly fought battleground, and I, along with most of the press gallery, had taken a keen interest not only in the policy itself but in the man Whitlam had chosen to turn the dream into reality.

On the face of it, he was an unlikely choice. William George Hayden was not exactly a political veteran; he had first been elected in 1961 and, while considered a member of the Left, had always exhibited a somewhat quirky independence. He had a disarming sense of humour and an appealing lack of pomposity; while passionate about his politics and utterly dedicated to the Labor cause, he could also recognise the occasional absurdities of the system.

We were on friendly terms, so when the full ministry was finally sworn in I went around to his new office to congratulate him and see how he was settling in. Hayden himself was not there, but his staff were struggling with the logistics of the place. Hayden's new principal adviser, P. P. McGuinness, then about halfway along his transition between student anarchist and perverse reactionary (and thus somewhere round the Whitlamite centre), was struggling to open the massive cast-iron safe with which the office was equipped.

Paddy and I knew each other – I had once bailed him out of jail following an anti-apartheid demonstration – and he turned to me for help: 'Have a go at this,' he said, handing me a piece of paper with the combination on it. 'I can't make it work.' I got the safe open; passing bureaucrats were aghast at this appalling breach of security, which clearly confirmed all their worst suspicions abut the recklessness of the new government.

But that was how things were at the time: we knew each other, we trusted each other, and it was time to let some fresh air into a system which had passed into an advanced state of decay. Hayden, when I told him the story later, thought it was a hoot; he had never been reluctant to challenge shibboleths that had outlived their usefulness.

This was obvious from his early days in the party, when, as a young former policeman elected as a delegate to the Queensland state conference, he found himself pitted against the state's legendary hard man, Jack Egerton. Hayden wanted to ban professional boxing and decriminalise homosexuality. Egerton summed up his position by saying: 'Delegate Hayden seems confused. He's bitterly opposed to a bloke getting a punch on the nose but he doesn't seem to mind him getting a punch up the bum.' When Hayden insisted on a vote on the issue, Egerton invited the men to go to one side of the room and the poofters to the other.

In spite of these setbacks, Hayden won preselection for the Liberal-held seat of Oxley and won it. Menzies ridiculed him as 'a poor little ignoramus' and 'the boy delinquent from Queensland', but in fact he stood out as one of the more diligent and original backbenchers and reached the front bench in 1969, becoming shadow minister for social security. When he assumed the portfolio after the 1972 election, the Ipswich copper became a political superstar.

The campaign against the Medibank reforms by sections of the medical profession and their allies on the Coalition benches was arguably the most vicious and unscrupulous in Australian political history. Hayden was regularly portrayed as a Nazi, in charge of the SS (social security) department dedicated to the extermination of both doctors and patients. Rumours were spread that he had broken down and was under psychiatric care; his wife, Dallas, received more than one phone call informing her that her husband was now confined to an institution. A lesser man would indeed have cracked, but somehow Hayden hung on until the relevant legislation was passed at the joint sitting of parliament after the 1974 election.

The success made him Whitlam's undisputed heir apparent within the parliamentary party, an assessment confirmed by his successful promotion as the government's last-hope treasurer. But when the leadership was offered after the wipeout of the dismissal, he declined it and took the opportunity to resume his studies. When he was finally ready in 1977, his time had effectively passed; a cloud no bigger than the undersized Bob Hawke was already looming on the Labor horizon. It is difficult to say what a Hayden government would have been like, but it is safe to say that it would have been a lot less predictable than the Hawke regime.

While Hayden had come a long way from the days when he used to startle guests by hiding in his office wardrobe until they had been seated and then bursting out insouciantly to warn them to prepare for an immediate fire drill, and while he no longer looked as if he had been dressed by a 1940s St Vincent de Paul shop, or talked as if he had been scripted by John Cleese, the hard fact remained that he was never able to take the pursuit and maintenance of power all that seriously, and certainly not power for its own sake.

It was probably this deeply sane attitude which led the satirist Patrick Cook to give him the nickname Will Winkie, a put-down which summed up perfectly the doubts that Labor's hard men had always retained about a man who never really fitted their mould. Hayden almost won in 1980 and would probably have won the drover's dog election of 1983, but he was denied the chance. Comparing himself to Shakespeare's anti-hero Macbeth, he accepted his fate and joined the Hawke government as its jet-setting foreign minister.

In private conversations with friends, the word Hayden most often used to describe the Hawke government was 'dull' – but after the high-wire act of the Whitlam years, that's how it was meant to be. Cabinet meetings were a bore, to be avoided at all costs. There was nothing in the way of intellectual cut and thrust, and radical or innovative ideas were ruthlessly crushed. Policies were predetermined by Hawke and his right-wing cronies and pushed through by a combination of thuggery and attrition. If Hayden had been in charge, it would all have been much more exciting …

No doubt. But the thought of a return to the excitement of the Whitlam days struck fear and loathing into the hearts of those ALP members lining up for their pension. There were times when the globetrotting foreign minister generated quite enough headlines on his own, even without being in charge of the whole shebang.

When Hayden assumed the vice-regal residence in 1988, with all the perks that went with it, there was something of a feeling of catharsis. At long last the debt had been paid. Just so long as Bill could confine his peculiar sense of humour to Boy Scout rallies, and not try and be too smart – at least not at the expense of the government ... And although he once rang me for advice on whether he should keep a flock of peacocks on the lawns at Yarralumla, on the whole his time as governor-general was uncontroversial. On retirement, the former republican surfaced briefly at the Constitutional Convention of 1998 to argue the case for the monarchy, before resuming his life as a gentleman farmer on the Darling Downs.

In his latter years Hayden has been seen by many of his colleagues as something of an eccentric – even as a bit of an opportunist. His claim to be keeper of the party's conscience, which he maintained for much of his parliamentary career, was seen to have been invalidated by his acceptance of that final job for the boy. He would never be considered a grand old man in the way Whitlam still was by the dwindling band who remember what the dawn of 1972 was really like; instead, he was destined to become a kind of Fred Daly figure, or at best a Jim McClelland; a Labor gadfly whose day never quite came; Will Winkie at Yarralumla.

This was quite unfair, of course, both to Hayden the politician and to Hayden the man. As minister, Hayden undertook the mammoth task of rejigging a national health and welfare system that was both discriminatory and inequitable. As treasurer, he pulled together an economy which had gone off the rails (it should be remembered that Fraser adopted Hayden's 1975 budget unchanged). As opposition leader, he raised his party from its lowest ebb, returning it to the status of an alternative government.

He was a loyal friend and colleague whose loyalty was too seldom reciprocated when it mattered. He was an ideas man whose scepticism probably challenged the prevailing orthodoxy too often for his own good, and whose sense of the ridiculous never deserted him in a profession in which most take themselves far too seriously. His main fault was that, in the winner-takes-all school of Australian politics, he was not sufficiently megalomaniac.

There was a certain poignancy in the fact that Bill Hayden, the sensitive South Brisbane copper, the relentless self-improver, the kid with the fire in his belly who set out in his teens to change the country (if not the world) and played a significant role in the most important social and political changes of his generation, should now see the pompous and anachronistic irrelevance of Yarralumla (as he once more or less described it) as the pinnacle of his career; something of which his children and grandchildren can be proud. Perhaps they will, but I suspect that the Hayden kids absorbed enough of their father's reformist zeal to place his earlier achievements well ahead of his comfortable (dare one say self-indulgent?) semi-retirement.

But these days self-indulgence seems to be the go, so perhaps I may be permitted a few personal flashbacks. I remember Hayden as the firebrand minister for social security in 1972, who took on the entrenched forces of the medical profession and the private health funds and, after a year and a half of almost unendurable pressure and vilification, beat them.

I remember Hayden as an almost lone voice for economic numeracy in 1975, finally winning over his lemming-like colleagues to a policy which just might have saved the government if it had run its full term.

I remember Hayden's office after 11 November as the oasis to which loyalists flocked, working twenty-four hours a day in a desperate attempt to salvage something from the wreckage.

I remember Hayden at the time of the Hawke challenge, showing immense grace under pressure while his colleagues and the media turned against him.

I remember his peculiarly self-deprecatory humour (another Whitlam legacy?) as foreign minister, a job which even his enemies admit he did at least as well as any of his predecessors.

I remember his defence of his wife, Dallas, in the face of one of the nastiest personal attacks in living memory.

But most of all I remember sitting round the backyard of the Haydens' modest Ipswich house on a summer evening, indulging in the kind of old-fashioned political argument that has gone out of fashion.

And I'd rather keep the memories – not of H. E. the Hon. W. G. Hayden G. G. or of Will Winkie, but of plain Bill.

REX CONNOR

N ALL THE RICH MENAGERIE OF THE WHITLAM GOVERNMENT, few of the inhabitants were more noticeable than Reginald Francis Xavier Connor; none was more formidable. A huge, dour and intimidating man, he had lived through two World Wars and the Great Depression, had two convictions for assault behind him, and had abandoned a successful motor dealership for politics. Connor, universally known as Rex, cast a long shadow before, during and after his turbulent time as a minister. His achievements were considerable, but his fall was spectacular.

Like many of his colleagues, Connor came to Canberra via the cauldron of New South Wales state politics; thirteen years on the government backbench in Macquarie Street had toughened him for the times that lay ahead. In those days he was considered a firebrand left-winger, suspiciously close to the Communist Party, but having gone federal, he modified his ideology, if not his bellicose approach. He attached himself to the rising star of Gough Whitlam and became a useful and dependable ally in Whitlam's long-running war with the party's self-styled left-wing old guard, although in his working-class electorate of Wollongong he maintained his power base.

He became Labor's spokesman in the emerging field of minerals and energy, and although he lost his position on the front bench after the 1969 election, he was the natural choice for the portfolio when the party took government. From the start, he made it clear that he would be satisfied with nothing less than a revolution in the area. This was in the days long before the mining boom, when mineral exports were regarded as something of a backwater, lightly taxed and generally the subject of cosy arrangements between buyers and sellers. Connor instituted export controls and forced the miners to insist on higher prices and longer contracts, which included hedges against inflation and currency variations. He also increased their taxes. He moved Australian iron ore into the emerging Chinese market and established a gas pipeline authority to bring gas from the Cooper Basin to south-eastern Australia; this was the precursor to a national grid, which would transform the country's energy supplies.

An aggressive nationalist, he liked to quote a piece of doggerel which turned out to be written by an obscure American named Sam Walter Foss:

> *Give me men to match my mountains,*
> *Give me men to match my plains.*
> *Men with freedom in their vision*
> *And creation in their veins.*

But the breadth and daring of his vision matched that of his leader, who loved the idea of big projects; Whitlam spoke wistfully of the need for something like the Suez Canal. Connor's pipeline grid looked like a good second best. But it would be fiendishly expensive, so cabinet hatched a somewhat harebrained scheme to borrow $4 billion (a huge amount in 1974) from the oil-rich sheikhs of the Middle East. A clearly shonky Pakistani carpetbagger called Tirath Khemlani emerged with promises of untold wealth, but failed to deliver; after a long and frustrating hiatus, during which the scheme was leaked to the opposition and became a media scandal, cabinet withdrew Connor's authority to negotiate.

But the minister did not give up; he secretly pursued the evanescent deal, and could often be found late at night, a disconsolate figure sitting by the teleprinter in his deserted office, hoping against hope for good news. His protégé Paul Keating was horrified: 'For God's sake, Rex,' he admonished, having sprung his mentor at one of these futile vigils. 'This is no way for a minister to behave.' And it wasn't, because Connor had assured parliament that he had ceased the negotiation. When it was discovered that he hadn't, Whitlam had no choice: misleading parliament was the unforgiveable crime, and Connor had to go.

But he was a big man, and his fall shook the earth. The opposition leader, Malcolm Fraser, quizzed by reporters about the likelihood of a repetition of the 1974 blocking of supply, had replied that he generally believed that governments had the right to serve their full term. But there was a caveat: an exception could be made if there were 'extraordinary and reprehensible circumstances'. Connor's dismissal could be, and was, parlayed into such a circumstance, and the rest was history.

It had the elements of tragedy, but also of farce, as did Connor's entire career. His apparently uncontrollable fits of temper had earned him the nickname 'The Strangler'; his staff played up the idea by hanging a noose above his office door to warn off unwary journalists. Connor thought it a great joke, but eventually the effort of playing the part got too much for him. Tired and embittered in opposition, he died while still a member of parliament in 1977. He wrote his own epitaph: life, said this larger-than-life figure, is an equation in hydrocarbons.

TOM UREN

F GOUGH WHITLAM HAD EVER NEEDED A BODYGUARD — AND there were many times when it seemed not a bad idea — one was always on tap: cabinet's gentle giant, Tom Uren. On his record, Uren, the quintessential militant lefty from Sydney's west, would have been more likely to flatten his leader than shelter him, but in fact the relationship was seldom less than amicable and at times even affectionate. 'I love the bastard when he gets sentimental,' Uren confided to me after one particularly moving Whitlam speech.

Tom Uren was a rich mix of paradoxes. He was a heavy-weight fighter and a dedicated pacifist; a prisoner of the Japanese and an international socialist; a Utopian idealist and a pragmatic political numbers man.

His political career peaked as minister for urban and regional development in the Whitlam government from 1972 to 1975, and as the Labor Party's deputy leader in the chaotic period of reconstruction that followed. But he regarded his whole life as a process of growth, in which politics was an

68

important part, but only a part. Unlike many of his colleagues, he never became obsessive and he never became bitter. As he said, he was a fighter, not a hater.

Uren started life as a Balmain boy, but his family moved to the seaside suburb of Harbord (now Freshwater) when he was five. Like many others, they faced tough times through the Depression and Uren left school at thirteen to help stretch the finances. He was a talented sportsman who could have excelled in several fields, but eventually decided to concentrate on boxing because of a family link. Many good judges saw him as a future heavyweight champion, but the war intervened.

Uren joined the artillery and was sent to Timor, where his unit surrendered in 1942. He remained a strong supporter of Timorese independence for the rest of his life, and was deeply unhappy at what he saw as the callous attitude of successive Australian governments to the Indonesian takeover of the island and subsequent atrocities.

Uren was sent to the infamous Thai–Burma railway, where he and his fellow prisoners were forced to work in brutal conditions. It was here that he became a socialist, or, as he preferred to call it, a collectivist. The camp commander, Weary Dunlop, ran the camp according to the dictum 'from each according to his ability, to each according to his need'. Uren always attributed the fact that Australian prisoners had a far higher survival rate than British to the observance of this socialist principle. Dunlop remained one of his heroes until Dunlop's death in 1993.

Remarkably, even in those circumstances Uren was able to distinguish the evils of Japanese militarism from the humanity of individual Japanese. When he was transferred to Japan towards the end of the war, he shared his Australian Red Cross parcels with underfed Japanese workers in the same factory.

On his return to Australia, Uren tried to resume his boxing career, but his health wasn't really up to it. He married, drifted through various manual jobs and finally decided to give boxing a last try in England. After more health problems he returned and continued to drift from job to job until he was taken on as a trainee executive by Woolworths, where he found he had an unexpected talent for personnel management and soon became a store manager. He was sent to Lithgow, where he joined the ALP just in time for the great split. After a series of epic tussles with the groupers, he won preselection for the safe seat of Reid and was elected in 1958.

He arrived in Canberra with his reputation as an effective organiser for the Left already well established, but found his views were too purist for the majority: he tended to talk in Marxist lingo, describing everything in terms of 'the struggle'. But he found a kindred soul in Jim Cairns, then emerging as the guru of the new Left. Uren adopted Cairns as his intellectual mentor, offering in return a measure of practical political protection to his somewhat unworldly idol. He was prepared to take second place to Cairns in the anti-Vietnam movement, although he undertook the bulk of the political organising. They formed an odd, and frequently lonely, couple. 'At least,' Uren said to his friend on one fraught occasion, 'we have each other.'

Both men were highly suspicious of the rise of Whitlam, and remained on the fringes of his crusade for power, although both were given prominent front-bench positions. Uren, to his surprise, received the ground-breaking portfolio of urban and regional development, which he tackled with increasing enthusiasm as it became clear that Labor was at last ready to return to government. His management skills made DURD one of the government's few unqualified successes; he was devastated when it was dismantled by Malcolm Fraser's government, and more devastated still when Bob Hawke's government failed to reinstate it.

His success in government, together with the fact that he had cooperated with Whitlam while retaining his own political position, won Uren the position of deputy leader in opposition. This gave him access to the VIP aircraft fleet, which he used to pursue his campaigns in favour of Aboriginal land rights and against uranium mining.

His relations with Whitlam became strained and, after the loans affair, Uren switched his support to Bill Hayden. After the 1977 election he lost the deputy leadership to Lionel Bowen.

Although Uren and Bob Hawke were traditional enemies and Uren had been highly critical of Hawke's failure to mobilise the union movement in 1975, he wavered towards Hawke, and held a number of meetings with Paul Keating, when he felt Hayden was compromising his position on uranium mining. But when Hawke won office in 1983, he not only refused to revive DURD but removed housing from Uren's portfolio, leaving him with the junior portfolio of territories and local government. After the 1984 election, he lost territories, too.

During this period, Uren fought a rearguard action against uranium mining that made him very unpopular with the pragmatic Hawke. In the meantime, other members of the Left, led by Brian Howe, were transforming the faction into one more flexible and pragmatic in order to make it relevant to the consensus Hawke demanded. Uren was slowly frozen out and retired to the backbench in 1987. He left parliament in 1990 amid universal respect. He had been tough, but he had never been mean.

In retirement, he cultivated many friendships, especially with the painter Lloyd Rees. He built a house back in Balmain and tended his garden; he used to boast that in his garden, plants from all over the world coexisted in harmony. He became something of a father figure and mentor to one of the new generation of Labor hopefuls, Tanya Plibersek. He continued to agitate on behalf of Aborigines, the people of East Timor, and returned prisoners of war from the Japanese camps. He will be remembered as a model of personal political integrity. Australia has produced politicians who were cleverer, wittier, more polished and more sophisticated, but few if any have been more decent.

FRED DALY

L IKE HIS OLD FRIEND AND COLLEAGUE CLYDE CAMERON, Fred Daly was a long-term political foe of Gough Whitlam who became improbably reconciled with his leader in government. But unlike Cameron, Daly did not have a subsequent falling-out with Whitlam, nor did he pursue a vendetta. Because unlike Cameron, Daly was never a hater; deep down, he wanted to be everyone's friend. And in the end, he and Whitlam formed something of a jolly comedy duo, appearing in tandem and swapping gags with each other at the expense of the real opposition. You almost expected their interviews to end with the traditional *boom, tish*.

Frederick Michael Daly did not really write memoirs; he wrote anecdotes. And it is a measure of his political longevity that he was able to update his first volume – *From Curtin to Kerr* – and turn it into *From Curtin to Hawke*. If he had lived a little longer, there is no doubt he would have used Paul Keating to restore the alliteration.

Politics was his entire life, and he never really retired from it. Perhaps his real problem was that, somewhere about 1966, the political mainstream left him. In one sense his political career spanned at least seventy of his eighty-three years, but in another it fell into a series of separate episodes, many of them spectacular but none entirely satisfactory.

Daly's great strength was in his resilience: like his parliamentary antagonist and personal friend Jim Killen, he was capable of tumultuous passion, but never of sustained hatred. His killer instinct was finely honed, but it was a weapon to be used in the heat of battle and then returned to its sheath until the next serious outbreak of hostilities. If he had been more determined and single-minded, he might have gone further, but then he would never have maintained so many friendships, and he would certainly not have been Fred Daly.

Daly cut his political teeth in the Depression years, and his Irish larrikinism made it easy for him to identify with the battlers. He was always suspicious of wealth, power and privilege, and was firmly identified with the Left when he entered parliament under the slogan, 'Give us this day our Daly, Fred'. In 1943 Clyde Cameron, who shared his beliefs but was a far more Machiavellian figure, marked the young Daly as a man to watch.

Daly was in awe of John Curtin but related immediately to Ben Chifley, who became something of a father figure to him, as Chifley did to many young Labor members at the time. He was devastated when Chifley lost government in 1949, and more devastated by the leader's death less than two years later. He was prepared, somewhat reluctantly, to

74

support Doc Evatt for a time, although even then he felt much more comfortable with the idea of Arthur Calwell – but his allegiance changed forever during the critical caucus meeting of 20 October 1954.

Evatt's right-wing opponents moved a leadership spill. Daly voted with the majority to defeat the motion, but then, as he recalls it, 'Eddie Ward, a real hater, called for a division. To everyone's amazement Evatt leaped onto the table, pencil and paper in hand, red faced and excited, and triumphantly called out, "Get their names, get their names!" – It was a degrading and disgusting spectacle – twenty-eight members lined up like Japanese war criminals by colleagues with hate, vindictiveness and triumph written all over their faces.'

Daly and a few others joined the twenty-eight as a result. Evatt remained as leader, but with dwindling support. From then on Daly was identified with the Calwell camp, which represented the Right – or at least that part of the Right which did not split off to form the DLP.

The long years in opposition did little to change Daly's views; his nostalgia for the Chifley years was obvious. As a result, when Gough Whitlam began to steer the party in a different direction in the late 1960s, Daly was clearly identified with the old guard.

Under Whitlam, Daly became shadow minister for immigration, but there was a proviso: Whitlam insisted that Daly should not use his position to push for Labor's traditional White Australia Policy, which had already been officially abandoned by the Coalition government under Harold Holt. Daly, already antagonistic to Whitlam, defied the instruction and was demoted. It seemed briefly that his long career was coming to an end before really reaching a climax.

But Whitlam's victory in 1972 saw both caucus and the prime minister ready to use the veteran's undoubted talents. Daly's long electoral experience was put to work as minister for services and property, which meant he was in charge of electoral law reform. Perhaps more importantly, his years in the parliament were rewarded with his appointment as leader of the house, which put him in charge of the government's program and tactics.

He was an inspired choice. A natural debater for whom style was more important than content, Daly was fast, funny and devastatingly effective. Like his old mates Eddie Ward and Les Haylen, he could have an opponent squirming with embarrassment one moment and roaring with laughter the next.

He had many memorable moments; perhaps the best of all was a speech during the disastrous loans affair of 1975, when his party's fortunes were approaching rock bottom. The opposition had mounted a cloak-and-dagger operation to bring to Australia the shonky money dealer Tirath Khemlani, in the hope that he might incriminate Whitlam along with Jim Cairns and Rex Connor. Khemlani's stay in Canberra became a sort of *Keystone Cops* affair, which Daly sent up mercilessly. But like most of his best performances, in the end it was irrelevant: shortly afterwards the government was dismissed, and Daly's parliamentary life finally ground to a halt.

But not, of course, his political life. He was in great demand as an after-dinner speaker, and later as an author, and if he became something of a political anachronism as time went on, it did nothing to diminish his popularity. Sometimes the stories grated on modern ears: his account of the 1949 election campaign, when he attacked the Jewish background of an opponent, does not make comfortable reading. But generally his good humour stopped anyone from taking offence.

In his later years Daly began yet another career, that of tour guide. He had long since deserted his inner-Sydney roots for the leafier suburbs of Canberra, and decided to capitalise on his knowledge of the place. Daly's tours took busloads of visitors around the political highlights of the national capital: the places where plots had been hatched, blunders unmasked and careers blighted. Daly himself provided the commentary, and if it sometimes became a trifle unreliable, who was to know or complain? Like his friend Jim Killen, Daly had become a political institution in his own right.

But it is hard to believe that his life story was quite the way he would have planned it as a young fire-eater during the turmoil of the Lang era in New South Wales, when injustice was there to be conquered and the world seemed ripe for changing. Trapped in the seemingly endless Menzies years, Daly was the wrong man in the wrong time when Labor finally regained government.

He became the government's ultimate political spruiker, a talent he took into retirement. It is as a spruiker, not as an innovator or reformer, that he will be affectionately remembered.

FRANK CREAN

TO MOST OUTSIDERS, FRANK CREAN WAS ONE OF THE LEAST distinguished members of the Whitlam mob. True, he was a senior minister, taking over the key treasury portfolio as soon as the full ministry was elected. In theory he should have been one of the most powerful and vocal of the new government's front bench, promoting its policies and putting the argument for the increases in government spending needed to finance them. But in practice he was never among the movers and shakers, preferring a background role. When he was eventually replaced as treasurer by the far better known Jim Cairns, all the attention was on the newcomer; Crean spent the rest of his career in comfortable obscurity.

It need not have been thus; Crean had the potential to be one of Labor's brightest stars and was even talked about as a future leader in the days before Whitlam made his own claims for the job irresistible. Whitlam himself once remarked to his then leader, Arthur Calwell, that between them, he and Crean outshone the entire government front bench. Obviously Whitlam believed that he himself provided the superior source of lumens, but it says a lot for Crean that the brash young pretender would even mention him in the same breath.

Francis Daniel Crean was that rare hybrid, an Irish Presbyterian. He identified with Labor's Left, as Victorians pretty much had to following the great split of the 1950s, but was in fact the nearest thing to a neutral in the factional wars. He had no real enemies in the caucus, which he joined in 1951 after a stint in Victorian state politics. This was one of the reasons he rose rapidly through the ranks, being elected to the front bench in 1956; the other was that he had been through Melbourne University and, rarer still, had a commerce degree and had practised as an accountant. In the Labor caucus of the 1950s, this was the equivalent of a Nobel prize in economics, and Crean immediately became the opposition's financial spokesman – in effect, the shadow treasurer, although the position was not formalised until 1969.

There was never really any doubt that he would take over as treasurer when Labor finally regained office, although by then others – notably Jim Cairns and Bill Hayden, both genuine economics graduates – felt they had superior qualifications. And Crean got through his first two budgets without serious controversy, although by the second, in 1974, inflation was already seriously out of control. Ironically, the accountant in him distrusted the orthodox advice he was getting from Treasury officials, but he did not feel he had the authority to challenge it, and the more than doubling of the price of oil ended up derailing the Australian economy. Whitlam, intent on implementing his reform program while there was still time, simply ignored the warning signs.

It may have been something of a relief when Cairns, having taken the job of deputy prime minister, demanded Treasury as his due. And in the end Crean had a sort of revenge: when Whitlam sacked Cairns for misleading parliament, Crean, having already taken Cairns' old portfolio of trade, replaced his usurper as deputy prime minister. However, before long the dismissal put an end to all their ambitions. In opposition Crean stood unsuccessfully against Whitlam for the leadership, and retired from politics in 1977.

But the family tradition lived on. One son, David, became a minister in the Tasmanian state Labor government and another, Simon, was president of the ACTU before entering the federal parliament in 1990. There he surpassed his father, serving as opposition leader and later as a senior minister in the governments of Kevin Rudd and Julia Gillard. It was easy to dismiss the Creans as a family of political plodders, but it was much harder to deny their very real achievements, both in and out of office.

KIM BEAZLEY

W HEN KIM EDWARD BEAZLEY WON A BY-ELECTION FOR
the seat of Fremantle following the death of John
Curtin in 1945, he was the youngest member of
parliament, just twenty-eight years old. He was
known as 'the Student Prince'. Thirty years later he became
the longest-serving member of the House of Representatives, the father of the parliament. Yet in all that time he had
been in government for just seven years and a minister for
barely three of them.

It would have been enough to embitter most politicians,
and many of his colleagues saw in Beazley a sour and occasionally vindictive man, typified by his much-quoted epithet:
'When I first joined the Labor Party, it was made up of the
cream of the working class. When I left it, it was made up of
the scum of the middle class.' But he remained loyal, idealistic and true to his deepest principles, and as education minister in the Whitlam years he was responsible for two of the
government's most far-reaching and popular reforms:

needs-based funding for all schools, whether government, church or private, and free university education. He would probably regret the way that both these changes have been watered down by governments from both sides of politics since, but he would always be proud to be the minister who introduced them.

Beazley was never less than a formidable figure in the party. At one stage he had been touted as successor to Arthur Calwell, but he was considered too uncompromising and right-wing by most of the caucus; the more telegenic Whitlam seemed the safer bet. Beazley held no grudges and became a steadfast ally of Whitlam against the old Left apparatus that dominated the party machine. As a West Australian delegate to the party's federal executive, he became a vital vote in the conflicts of the '60s and '70s, but never a solely partisan one: following his adherence to the harsh and unforgiving code of Moral Rearmament, which he had embraced as a student, Beazley insisted that everything should be done according to the rules not only of the party, but of natural justice. Even his most dedicated ideological opponents acknowledged his rectitude.

But it was not an endearing characteristic, and within caucus – indeed, within parliament – Beazley was a generally lonely figure. On the floor of the house, however, he was invariably an elegant and eloquent performer, a parliamentarian who could compete with Whitlam. A teetotaller (of course), he had plenty of time for research, which he used against his less erudite opponents to devastating effect. I remember one speech in which he gave Billy Snedden a lecture on Russian history that made the then opposition leader look like a humiliated schoolboy.

In the end, his principles were simply too severe for politics. In 1976 the news broke that Whitlam had been involved in negotiations to raise a loan from the Ba'ath Socialist Party of Iraq to pay off the party's debts, causing Beazley to resign from the Labor front bench. The following year he left the parliament altogether, one of the few members of whom the appellation 'honourable' could be applied without irony.

And his legacy endured: as with his old friend Frank Crean, Beazley was in a sense surpassed by his son. Kim Junior became not only a very senior minister and deputy prime minister, but led his party for several years in opposition. The fact that he never won the top job would not have worried his father, who always held that being right was more important than material success. Whitlam, of course, would have disagreed; but that was why he was prime minister and Kim Beazley wasn't.

AL GRASSBY

THE WHITLAM YEARS THREW UP MANY COLOURFUL characters, but none outshone (either metaphorically or chromatically) Albert Jaime Grassby.

He was, surely, the first minister in Australian history to be sworn in wearing a bright purple suit, and the first to become the subject of a pop song which briefly reached the top forty.

His opponents derided him as a weed: Paterson's Curse, a vivid flowering plant (purple, of course) that tends to take over in uncultivated paddocks. Pretty but useless, the then National Party leader Doug Anthony proclaimed. But the irrepressible Grassby promptly reminded him that in times of drought, Paterson's Curse is also known as Salvation Jane, the last remaining fodder for desperate stock.

Grassby was never loath to portray himself as the saviour of rural Australia, the heroic knight at the fore of what he called the Crusade for the Countryside – this notwithstanding that he represented the Riverina district of southern

New South Wales, one of the lushest in Australia.

It was also one of the most culturally diverse. Grassby, a self-proclaimed citizen of the world who had lived on three other continents as a child before returning to Australia, found another cause in the promotion of the ideal of multi-culturalism – although he himself preferred the word poly-ethnicity, which unsurprisingly never caught on.

Multiculturalism had of course been creeping up on Australia for many years: since the postwar policy of Ben Chifley and Arthur Calwell of encouraging migration from southern as well as northern Europe, the old shibbo-leth of a predominantly British Australia had been pro-gressively undermined. In 1966 Harold Holt had formally signed off from the White Australia Policy, one of the great Australian socio-political planks which had endured since Federation. The Labor Party, previously the great protector of the policy, now went even further: under Gough Whitlam, Australia was to adopt a deliberate pol-icy of multiracialism. From this, of course, flowed multi-culturalism, and almost by accident Grassby found himself as its political face.

Grassby entered federal parliament in 1969 with a huge swing in what had been seen as Country Party heartland. The Murrumbidgee Irrigation Area, a cornucopia of wheat, citrus fruit and, increasingly, wine, was anything but tradi-tional Labor territory.

But Grassby, using the provincial centre of Griffith as his power base, broke all the rules. In a real sense he was the predecessor of what is now marketed as Country Labor, a sort of subgroup within the Labor Party that enjoys special privileges and makes its own rules.

His appearance in Canberra was greeted with both amusement and alarm; the old hardheads of the Country Party saw him as no more than a flashy aberration, and believed that he would quickly self-combust and give them back their lost territory as the sparks were extinguished. But they could not deny his vote-catching ability, or the charisma which drew the media to him in a way the sturdy traditionalists had never managed.

He rode his first term on the crest of a publicity wave; I recall one feature in which a reporter desperate for a metaphor waxed lyrical over the Riverina pastures, 'where the wheat is as high as the opal pin in Al Grassby's tie'.

When he was returned in 1972 as one of the more prominent members of the incoming Whitlam government, it was obvious he had to be found a place in the ministry – but where?

Theoretically, primary industry was the obvious portfolio; he was, after all, one of the very few Labor members with a genuine rural background. But there were problems: he was seen as too exuberant, too much of a loose cannon for what was still largely a conservative community. The party's chief backroom adviser on rural matters, Tom Connors, a journalist with the *Financial Review* in Canberra, simply refused to countenance him.

Eventually the job went to Ken Wriedt, a former seaman from Tasmania, who had absolutely no experience in the area but could be relied upon to follow Connors' guidance. In what was seen at the time as a consolation prize, Grassby was awarded the comparatively junior ministry of immigration.

If he was disappointed, he certainly didn't show it. He himself, he boasted, was something close to the archetypal migrant: a blend of races, nationalities and cultures which was typical of modern Australia, although many remained uncomfortable with the fact and chose to hide it. Instead, preached Grassby, we should glory in it: with the possible exception of the United States in the years immediately after the First World War, Australia was the first country to have opted for this kind of polyethnicity as a matter of conscious policy. Others had had multiracial immigration thrust upon them; we had embraced it by choice and should celebrate it.

Grassby was not responsible for the policy itself, which had, in a sense, been introduced by stealth – a stealth which some older Australians still resented. But he was its greatest propagandist and proselytiser, and by and large he was successful. People still grumbled in pubs about the influx of unfamiliar faces and voices, but for a long time they agreed that the change was not only inevitable, but in some way, which they found hard to articulate, the right thing. It was not until some twenty-five years later, when John Howard declared the bigotry of Pauline Hanson to be an acceptable part of public debate and exploited the arrival of asylum seekers as a threat to Australia, that the consensus of which Grassby was such an important part was seriously threatened.

Grassby in parliament was at least as flamboyant as he had been out of it. His talent for self-promotion was shameless: on frequent occasions he held extravagant parties for his colleagues in Canberra featuring the wines of the Riverina or, as their critics liked to describe them, vats of Murrumbidgee mud. On one such occasion, a new member confronted by an elaborate label asked innocently: 'Where's Shiraz?' Richie Gun, a genuine wine buff from South Australia, replied wearily: 'I'm sitting on it.'

The Grassby hospitality was even more lavish in his electorate, where he and his wife, Ellnor, held huge picnics-cum-barbecues to which it seemed the whole world had been invited. Leaving one such function, Margaret Whitlam remarked, as she crunched several cubic metres of chicken bones underfoot, that it had been something like attending a cannibal feast.

It all added to the Grassby notoriety; it was around this time that the song 'Down in the Riverina' was written, or perhaps commissioned. It briefly made the charts, and included the line: 'It's Grassby country, you'll hear that all the time, when you're down in the Riverina.'

The problem was that it wasn't just Grassby country; it was also the turf of Robert Trimbole and his extended family, who were widely believed to run the burgeoning marijuana trade in the district and were close political allies of Grassby, who passionately defended them against their accusers. Long after he had left parliament, when Don Mackay, the anti-drug campaigning state MP, was murdered in 1977, Grassby maintained that it was somehow his own fault, or at least that of his family.

This did not go down well. The descriptions of Grassby as 'the colourful government minister' started to acquire the same connotation as 'colourful racing identity' had in the crime reports. He had always been seen as a bit of a spiv; now it became more serious.

In the snap election of 1974, he lost his seat. However, he was far from finished: he continued as a passionate advocate of multiculturalism (as he now resignedly called it) and an even more fervent opponent of racism and bigotry. Although he was an Australian patriot on his own terms, he railed against the more strident nationalism of later years, which he saw as a shallow excuse for jingoism or, still worse, the basis for some fuzzy idea of Australians as the new master race.

It was always his wish, and his belief, that Australia should become the most successful multicultural society in the world. Today, even conservatives, John Howard included, would argue that it has become just that. If they are right, then Grassby deserves his share of the credit.

JIM McCLELLAND

N THE DESPERATE DAYS OF 1975, GOUGH WHITLAM SOUGHT TO surround himself with stalwarts, longstanding supporters he could trust to back him no matter what. Unsurprisingly, he turned to Jim McClelland, an old legal colleague from the coterie that also produced, among others, Sir John Kerr. It is not known whether Whitlam imagined the latter connection might be helpful, but it is certain that McClelland, whatever his other tergiversations, was and always remained a devout Whitlamite. When Whitlam, with some difficulty and after a nasty public brawl, finally ejected Clyde Cameron from his beloved industrial relations portfolio, McClelland was the obvious choice to fill the controversial post. He held the fort with stoic determination until the end.

It seems strange to describe 'Diamond' Jim McClelland as, really, rather an old-fashioned man. Few men of his generation displayed anything like his energy, his forthrightness, his optimism, or, most of all, his receptivity to new ideas. But if there was a continuous thread in his extraordinarily full and complex life, it can probably best be summed up as a very untrendy, passionate commitment to morality. The catch was that his idea of what constituted morality – or of what was the best way of achieving it – went from here to there and back again.

McClelland started as a devout and guilt-ridden Roman Catholic. Like many such, he developed doubts, and embraced communism in its most radical (and unachievable) form: Trotskyism. The doubts resurfaced; he became a dedicated fellow traveller of the Catholic-based Movement, committed to breaking the power of the communists within the unions. This in turn became unsatisfactory (or perhaps just boring) and the Camelot held out by the Labor Party under Whitlam's leadership beckoned.

Nineteen seventy-five disposed of that magnificent obsession, which was followed by a term in the Land and Environment Court, in which McClelland became greener than many of the greenies appearing before him. This obsession lasted him through the Royal Commission into British Nuclear Tests at Maralinga in 1983–85; about the same time, he became a convert to feminism.

An unkind critic would say that Diamond Jim had had more 'isms' than most of us have had hot breakfasts, and that a number of them – particularly the later ones – were suspiciously convenient for his career path at the time. But this would be neither fair nor true. At various times in his life, it was possible to label McClelland left or right, socialist or elitist, libertarian or authoritarian. But, as he pointed out himself with a touch of complacency, none of the labels really fitted. He was genuinely unclassifiable, which is what made him such an interesting and engaging – if at times infuriating – political figure.

His idiosyncratic morality explained much of the contradictory nature of the man. He was superficially gregarious: Diamond Jim surrounded by his mates of the moment was always an awe-inspiring sight. But the mates seldom lived up to the standards McClelland set for himself and, by implication, for them. His split with John Kerr – ironically, one of the people who suggested he enter parliament in the first place – was legendary. Even more than Whitlam, McClelland took the dismissal of 1975 as a personal betrayal. But the wayside of McClelland's life was littered with the bodies of other one-time close friends and important influences whom he had, in his own view at least, outgrown. His Trotskyist mentors, his right-wing unionist colleagues, his political benefactors – when he got around to writing his memoirs, appropriately entitled *Stirring the Possum*, there were few kind words for any of them.

Whitlam escaped more or less unscathed, although McClelland condemned his political judgement for having desperately reshuffled the ministry towards the apocalyptic end of his government. Bill Hayden received an approving nod. Another old mate, Neville Wran, was seen as something of a sellout. The Hawke/Keating government was dismissed as lacking both principle and style – the latter, in a funny way, being somewhat more important than the former. Indeed, it wasn't even a real Labor government. McClelland marked his report cards hard.

So, in the end, what were his consistent criteria? Intellectual rigour, certainly: he claimed to have read the whole of Karl Marx's *Capital* not once but twice (something few, if any, Australians can have managed) before parting company with communism. A desire for a more equal society, perhaps: the McClelland family weathered the Depression better than many, but his social-reforming zeal was a constant, although it went in many different directions. The pursuit of excellence also came into it: despite his nickname, McClelland had no time for drones or fools.

The last chapter of his book provided another insight: we needed geniuses, he declared, but even more we needed people who were prepared to embrace a cause. Why McClelland's causes were more worthwhile than others, we weren't told. But like his former leader, McClelland was seldom troubled by self-doubt.

Which brings us back to the old-fashioned aspects of this most energetically modern of thinkers. Our finest historian, Manning Clark, has written that ours was the first generation in history to have grown up without the idea of God. McClelland, with all respect, was really a member of the previous generation. He ended up a convinced atheist (he would never be so mealy-mouthed as to proclaim himself an agnostic) but throughout his life he had a relatively untroubled belief in God-substitutes: his causes. He was never unmotivated or despairing, and seldom bored.

Perhaps his brief time in the Whitlam government was the only period in which his didactic refusal to compromise with what he saw as cowardice and incompetence was a real disadvantage. In Australian terms, Diamond Jim was never really cut out to be a politician. Perhaps he saw himself more as a philosopher king, but Australians have never really taken to the idea.

The story of Diamond Jim, the boy from Richmond whose ambition, as he once said, was never to be rich but simply to be 'not poor', is at one level a success story, at another an enticing piece of social and political history, at another a disturbingly honest account of a man whose beliefs never quite fitted the world around him, and finally something of a morality play. If Diamond Jim had not existed, it would have been necessary to invent him.

DON WILLESEE

WHEN GOUGH WHITLAM AND LANCE BARNARD ENDED THEIR hectic duumvirate at the end of 1972 and Whitlam somewhat reluctantly allocated ministries to his colleagues, there were few surprises at the top. Whitlam kept foreign affairs in addition to the prime ministry. Barnard took defence, Frank Crean the Treasury, Kim Beazley education, Bill Hayden social security and Clyde Cameron labour. Lionel Murphy became attorney-general. But his deputy in the Senate, Don Willesee, wound up with a grab bag: special minister of state, vice-president of the executive council, minister assisting the prime minister and minister assisting the minister for foreign affairs.

It looked like a bit of a put-down for the man who was, on paper at least, the fourth-most senior in the government. But in fact it was an acknowledgement of the trust Whitlam placed in the unassuming Western Australian. With the mammoth workload he was taking on, the new prime minister knew he needed someone utterly reliable to look after the nuts and bolts of the job, and Willesee was the obvious choice.

Willesee had been waiting for government even longer than Whitlam himself. A staunch Labor man all his life, he had risen through the ranks of the Union of Postal Clerks and Telegraphists to become state secretary and later president. In 1950, after Ben Chifley lost office, he became the youngest member of the Senate at the age of thirty-four, only to spend the next twenty-three years in opposition.

He made many friends on both sides of the chamber, among them John Gorton, whose accession to the Lodge he applauded; but he did feel the need to warn Gorton that his flamboyant behaviour might lead to an early crash, which indeed it did. Willesee was no wowser, but he always believed that political proprieties had to be observed.

Largely by virtue of his seniority, he came to play a leading role in the affairs of the parliamentary party. In 1967 he briefly became the opposition Senate leader, only to lose that place to Lionel Murphy later in the same year. When the deputy leader Sam Cohen died in 1969, Willesee was elected in his place. This was especially important to Whitlam, who was then engaged in his campaign to reform the party structure. With the four parliamentary leaders admitted to the all-powerful national executive, Willesee was a vital vote on his side.

In government, Willesee maintained the low profile he had always held, but behind the scenes he was constantly on the move. One of Whitlam's first acts was to recognise the

People's Republic of China and initiate diplomatic relations; it was Willesee who worked through the complicated and sensitive details. Australia was taking a leading role in organising boycotts against the apartheid regime in South Africa; Willesee made a whirlwind tour of the continent, explaining the new position to often sceptical black African leaders. As relations with the South Pacific were upgraded, Willesee travelled the region, allaying worries among the island nations that Australia was attempting a form of neo-colonialism. During that first year he had little to do with policy, but was the key figure in its implementation.

At the end of 1973, Whitlam was finally persuaded to give up his second portfolio and Willesee was sworn in as minister for foreign affairs. As Whitlam still insisted on overseeing all foreign policy, the bonds between the two became a little more strained: the ambitious Whitlam became impatient with his colleague's native caution. None-theless, they seldom clashed.

One major disagreement was over Whitlam's decision in 1974 to try to take control of the Senate by appointing the DLP veteran Vince Gair to a diplomatic post. Willesee felt this was both politically risky and ethically dubious, but it was pushed through while he was on an official trip to America. The fact that his judgement was spectacularly vindicated did not help his relationship with Whitlam. The two also clashed over the admission of refugees from South Viet-nam; Willesee favoured a far more generous approach than Whitlam. Whitlam was also unimpressed when Willesee began sounding out support for the presidency of the United

Nations. But the government fell before any open breach between the two men could take place.

Interestingly, when the split did come, it was many years later, in the course of one of the many media debates over that most persistent of Labor sores, East Timor. Whitlam dismissed Willesee's contribution to foreign policy as that of a 'forgettable and forgetful' minister. To many, this was unfair, ungracious and unworthy; Willesee had given Whitlam unswerving loyalty even when he believed his leader was wrong, and deserved better in return.

At least the two agreed over the less controversial issue of the National Library, which Willesee completely reorganised as a public educational resource. It remains perhaps the most fitting memorial to a modest and unassuming but deeply committed and utterly scrupulous Labor stalwart. In a government more remembered for its high-wire acts than for its diligence, Willesee was one of the most stable and conscientious of officers.

MOSS CASS

R EADERS OF THESE REMINISCENCES (ALL RIGHT, LET'S BE honest, this homage) might be tempted to conclude that I consider Gough Whitlam a paragon, a nonpareil without fault or foible. Not at all: there were times when the leader, both before and after he became prime minister, could be very irritating indeed.

For instance, at campaign meetings, there was always the risk that he would abandon the speech prepared for him, a rousing call to electoral arms designed to get the voters flocking triumphantly to the polls, in favour of an eye-glazing eighty-minute lecture on the need for constitutional reform, an exercise that turned his bored and bewildered supporters away in droves. His office staff particularly disliked the fact that, in moments of extreme stress, their leader would suddenly grind his teeth noisily and threateningly; nervous stenographers sometimes feared he was preparing to devour them in the manner of Hannibal Lecter.

But his most antisocial, politically incorrect characteristic was his irrational dislike of the vertically challenged. Whitlam did not go quite as far as the song suggests: 'Short people got no reason to live.' But he certainly believed that they had no right to be in his immediate vicinity, and that if they must intrude, they should know their place. This attitude produced constant tension between himself and Bob Hawke, who considered himself at least the equal of his towering antagonist; the antipathy increased when the press gallery started referring to Hawke as 'Little Caesar', an epithet Hawke supposed, incorrectly, had originated in Whitlam's office.

Another man who bore the brunt of Whitlam's prejudice was Richie Gun, a small but perfectly formed medico from Adelaide and, from 1969, the Labor member for Kingston. Whitlam regularly stomped on him in caucus, and was therefore both surprised and infuriated when he was shown an election pamphlet in which it was stated: 'Dr Gun has been frequently praised by Gough Whitlam for the depth and breadth of his knowledge.'

Whitlam called Gun in at once. 'I have never said any such thing,' he insisted loudly.

'Oh, yes, you have,' responded Gun. 'You have often called me a little fucking know-all.'

For once the leader was at a loss for words.

At least he did not have to put up with Gun in cabinet. However, there was no way Whitlam could avoid another medico, Moss Cass, the miniature member for Maribyrnong. Cass had been elected to the ministry, and so had to be confronted and even conversed with on a regular basis. To make it worse, Cass sported a rather natty beard, and Whitlam was a dedicated pognophobe. He put up with my own appendage, which he only encountered occasionally, but within his office, while he tolerated a considerable degree of scruffiness, complete facial depilation was the rule. But there was nothing he could do about Cass; and if all this wasn't enough, Cass continued to be an active member of the Victorian Socialist Left, Whitlam's most bitter opposition within the party. What was there to like about the man?

Well, quite a bit, actually. Cass was a member of the intellectual Jewish left, that peculiarly Melbourne institution which has contributed so much to the progressive cause over the years. Smart, savvy and deeply committed, his dedication to the Labor movement could never be questioned. And if his ideology was a bit extreme for the pragmatic political moderates, was the existence of a ginger group within caucus to remind them of their ultimate raison d'être such a bad thing?

I was of course first and foremost a Whitlamite, but my political instincts were still drawn to the left, and I found Cass an attractive figure. In particular, I sympathised with his impatience with the necessary but frequently tedious rituals that went with the job of being a parliamentarian. 'What am I doing here?' he complained to me once after a long day listening to particularly unexciting speeches. 'I'd rather be home fucking my wife.'

In fact, Bettina Cass, an activist in her own right, was a frequent visitor to Canberra; on one occasion she attended a tea party, hosted by Sonia McMahon for wives of politicians, bedecked with women's lib badges. Later, she wrote a gently sardonic account of the gathering, which we published in

Nation Review. Moss Cass likewise maintained his commitment to direct action; he was a regular at moratorium marches and peace rallies. When the Springbok rugby team played a match in Canberra in 1975, Cass joined the demonstrators at Manuka Oval, happily accepting one of the placards I was handing out. His selection, as I recall, was 'RUCK OFF RACISTS'.

Whitlam had hoped to hide Cass by making him minister for the environment, then a very junior portfolio discredited by its previous minister, the unloved and unlovely Peter Howson. Environment was still a fringe issue in those days, but Cass grabbed the opportunity to raise its profile. He lost more battles than he won – Lake Pedder was flooded and a transmission tower built on Canberra's Black Mountain, and some of his colleagues started referring to him as 'the Minister for Lost Causes'. But he revived John Gorton's campaign to gain control of and protect the Great Barrier Reef, and set in motion the machinery that later ended sand mining on Fraser Island. He also led the caucus opposition to uranium mining, his medical background giving him more authority than some of his less well-informed allies.

Most importantly, he constantly talked up the environmental cause both in and out of cabinet, winning a useful and enthusiastic supporter in Tom Uren in the process. In 1975 he had a crash-through moment almost worthy of Whitlam himself: Jim Cairns was removed as treasurer but remained as deputy prime minister, giving him the right to any other portfolio of his choice. Cass persuaded him to take over environment in an attempt to raise its profile. In the event, the tactic failed: soon afterwards, Cairns was sacked from the ministry altogether and, in the dying days of the government, a new minister, Joe Berinson, took over. But Cass had done his job: never again would the environment be treated as a fringe political issue.

Cass himself took over Doug McClelland's media portfolio and quickly set about giving it some serious clout. With the aid of his zealous staffer Henry Rosenbloom (who later became a notable publisher), he set up the Community Radio Network, which Malcolm Fraser later adopted as a model for SBS radio. Cass also suggested the formation of a voluntary press council, a move that provoked a ferocious and misleading backlash from the Murdoch press – the more things change, et cetera. His short time in the job was innovative and productive, and one would have liked it to go further. But like his stature, his time in office was short. He retired from politics in 1983 – the year Labor regained power – to pursue his passion for reform in other forums.

But Cass will always be remembered for one phrase which, in a slightly edited form, has gone into the environmental lexicon. In a speech to the OECD in Paris in 1974, he declared: 'We have not inherited this earth from our parents to do with it what we will. We have borrowed it from our children and we must be careful to use it in their interests as well as our own.' Not even the towering Gough Whitlam could have put it better.

JIM COPE

EVERYONE AGREED THAT JAMES FRANCIS COPE WAS A very nice bloke – and therefore entirely the wrong choice for speaker. A glassworker from Redfern, he had been elected to parliament in 1955 and had sat uncomplainingly on the back bench ever since. A hail-fellow-well-met type, he drank with colleagues and opponents alike and played snooker with anyone who would give him a game. In time he became the undisputed snooker champion of Parliament House, and it was generally believed that this was as high as he was destined to rise.

He spent a lot of time in the house and became known for his interjections. Perhaps the best of them came during the interminable debate over the new Parliament House and whether it should be situated on the site of the old one, or by the lake, or on Capitol Hill. As the argument dragged on into the early hours of the morning, one exasperated member made his way out of the chamber, pausing only to snarl: 'Well, as far as I'm concerned, you can stick it up your arse.'

Quick as a flash, Cope chimed in: 'Mr Speaker, I ask that the parliament consider the fourth site proposed by the honourable member.'

It was quips like this that persuaded the caucus to nominate him as their choice for speaker. In the long years in opposition, this did not matter because the government invariably succeeded in its own appointment. But then, suddenly, in 1972 the office and its considerable perks were theirs for the taking. It would have been churlish to dump Cope now – and his many friends, looking forward to long evenings enjoying his hospitality in the well-stocked speaker's suite, wouldn't have heard of it. So the diminutive figure of Jim Cope ascended the speaker's chair.

From the beginning, the Coalition opposition, and in particular the National Party head-kickers, Doug Anthony, Ian Sinclair and Peter Nixon, gave him hell. They ignored standing orders, dissented from his rulings and accused him of bias. With obvious reluctance, Cope decided it was time to switch from good cop to bad cop, and eventually invoked the ultimate sanction of suspending repeat offenders from parliament. But his heart was clearly not in it, and he became known in opposition ranks as Jim Can't Cope. The more he tried to play the tough guy, the more recalcitrantly they baited him, and eventually he cracked.

During one fiery debate in 1975, Clyde Cameron made remarks to which the opposition objected; they demanded a withdrawal. Cope, desperately trying to restore the peace, asked Cameron to withdraw; Cameron indignantly refused and Cope named him – the preliminary to suspension.

Seizing the opportunity, Sinclair moved the suspension immediately; standing orders meant that the motion had to be put at once, and without debate. But it was clear that Labor members were not going to vote to suspend one of their own, especially when they believed the original provocation had come from the other side. In the melee that followed, Whitlam approached Cope; it was later reported that he said: 'If this goes against you, you will have to resign.' From where I was sitting, it sounded more like: 'Now you've stuffed it and you'll have to resign.'

Cope sat stony-faced; when it was announced that the motion for suspension had been lost, he tendered his resignation immediately. Strictly, as the clerk later pointed out, he did not need to; there had been no formal motion of dissent or no confidence. But the amiable Cope had clearly had enough. His remaining time in parliament was not happy; he never really forgave his colleagues for deserting him, and when the dust settled, many of them found it hard to forgive themselves.

The repercussions from that day endured; it could be said that Cope's resignation marked the moment that the government, and more importantly Whitlam, began to lose control of parliament. That in turn opened the path for Malcolm Fraser, who was considered more likely than the incumbent, Bill Snedden, to exploit the situation. And the Labor toboggan began its long and irreversible slide downhill.

THE REST

ONCE, WHEN GOUGH WHITLAM WAS ASKED IF HE WAS
embarrassed by so many of his ministers behaving
like prima donnas, the prime minister drew himself to his full and imposing height and thundered:
'I don't care how many prima donnas there are, as long as I
am Prima Donna Assoluta!'

Like many of his attempts at self-satire, it was mistaken
for arrogance by his critics and largely ignored by his supporters. But in fact the statement glossed over a troubling
fact: while the frontrunners in the Whitlam mob behaved
like superstars and did their best to live up to their self-
assessment, there was a long and undistinguished tail. The
middle-rankers were generally competent enough, but the
also-rans were generally very also indeed.

There was a handful who had the talent but were not
given the time or opportunity to develop it. Lionel Bowen,
an amiable, generally retiring graduate from the New South
Wales parliament, held only junior ministries under

Whitlam but survived to become deputy leader of the party under Bob Hawke and was even talked about for the top job. Paul Keating had barely been appointed minster for the Northern Territory in 1975 before being informed by his prime minister: 'You're sacked.' It took the bewildered newcomer some time to realise that it wasn't just him but the entire government. Mick Young, who as party secretary had been the principal architect of the 1972 victory strategy, won his seat in 1974 but did not reach the front bench until the party was back in opposition. Another who rose in the Whitlam aftermath was Barry Cohen, Whitlam's faithful chronicler.

But by and large it was a government with a large gap between the best and the rest. This is not to deny the value of some of the middle rankers: Rex Patterson, Ken Wriedt and Bill Morrison all handled difficult portfolios well; John Wheeldon in the Senate was a brilliant orator but always something of a dilettante. He eventually deserted Labor to go over to the dark side, joining the *Australian* as a leader-writer for Rupert Murdoch. Kep Enderby was an innovative attorney-general, but is more famous for announcing triumphantly, during a brief stint as stand-in trade minister: 'Traditionally, most of Australia's imports have come from overseas.' Joe Berinson and Joe Riordan both came to ministry late, but showed promise.

But then there was Charlie Jones, best known for having narrowly avoided a diplomatic incident when discussing fishing with the prime minister of Papua New Guinea, Michael Somare; asked his favourite fish, Jones replied without hesitation: 'Niggers.' He was an aficionado of the black bream. Frank Stewart is chiefly remembered for being suspected of leaking damaging details of the loans affair to Labor's opponents. Doug Everingham's stint in health was most famous for his efforts to institute spelling reform and for his anti-smoking campaign, which involved plastering the Parliament House cigarette vending machine with skull and crossbones stickers, an activity which got him into trouble with the house authorities. Gordon Bryant, Jim Cavanagh and Les Johnson were all ministers for Aboriginal affairs; enough said. And Reg Bishop used to plead not to be promoted; he had enough difficulty mastering the portfolio of postmaster-general without straining himself any further.

But probably the best known of the nonentities, to coin an oxymoron, was Doug McClelland, on no account to be confused with his more flamboyant namesake Diamond Jim. Rubber Dougie, as he was universally known, arrived in Canberra in 1961 and immediately hitched himself to the Whitlam bandwagon. An ex-serviceman turned reporter, he was a gregarious and uncomplicated type who made friends easily and immersed himself in committee work. His progress through the ranks was therefore assured and he was elected to the first Whitlam ministry pretty much automatically. But then there was the problem of what to do with him. On discovering that McClelland had maintained his membership of the Australian Journalists' Association, Whitlam created a ministry for the media and slotted his old ally into it.

The media, on the whole, were less than impressed; even the famous comedian Graham Kennedy joined a chorus demanding that McClelland be sacked and the ministry abolished. But the senator persevered, and had at least one triumph: after he introduced a points system for television programming that had an unfavourable impact on the coverage of Aussie Rules, the Anti-Football League awarded him its highest honour, the Douglas Wilkie medal. In 1975 he added the title of special minster of state to his portfolio, but that was a far as he went. After the dismissal he remained in the Senate, but did not return to the ministry under Bob Hawke. Instead, he was given the consolation prize of the Senate presidency, having already become its longest-serving member in 1981.

He retired from parliament in 1987 and promptly took up an appointment as Australia's high commissioner to the UK, picking up a Companionship of the Order of Australia on the way through. And in the best Labor tradition he founded a dynasty, of a kind: his son Robert is a lawyer who was elected to parliament in 1996 and served four years as attorney-general during the Rudd/Gillard years.

And that was Rubber Dougie, not the best, brightest or most spectacular of the Whitlam ministers, but one of the foot soldiers – the kind of spear carrier the prima donnas need to fill up the stage. It can at least be said that he and most of his fellow extras fulfilled their roles without seriously embarrassing the audience, which is rather more than can be said for some of the stars.

DON DUNSTAN

G OUGH WHITLAM'S SHORT TIME IN OFFICE WAS BESET BY enemies on all sides, but few were as damaging as the conservative premiers. From start to finish his government was at war with the eastern-staters. There was Robert Askin in New South Wales, and Joh Bjelke-Petersen was well into his hillbilly dictatorship in the deep north. In Victoria Rupert Hamer had succeeded the terminally recalcitrant Sir Henry Bolte, but the latter's long, broad, ultra-conservative shadow still enveloped the state. In the beginning there was some aid and comfort to be had from the minor states, but in 1974 Labor's John Tonkin lost office in Western Australia and shortly afterwards Eric Reece succumbed in Tasmania.

Only South Australia remained in the fold, but in some ways that compensated for all the rest, because the premier of that generally benighted state was the extraordinary, the unique Donald Allan Dunstan, a like-minded progressive and moderniser who in some ways played the role of John the Baptist to Whitlam's Messiah. The two men were rational optimists with a shared belief in the essential intelligence and goodness of humanity, natural enlargers in contrast to the punishers and straiteners who preceded and succeeded them. One of the many things they had in common was a somewhat quirky sense of humour.

One of Don Dunstan's favourite stories concerned a pianist of Chinese ancestry performing the works of Franz Liszt before a very upper-class English audience.

After the concert, he was sought out by a gushing admirer. 'Oh, Mr Chang,' she enthused, 'I do think it's wonderful that someone of your race should have such a feeling for our music.' To which the pianist replied, 'Really, Lady Fortescue, I had no idea you were Hungarian.'

Much of Dunstan is there: the familiarity with the arts, the loathing of racial stereotyping, the delight in pricking pomposity. Much, but by no means all. But it was this aspect of Dunstan that most people latched on to: the naughty boy from Fiji who wore pink shorts into parliament simply to cock a snook at the establishment.

They saw, and either loved or hated, according to their politics, Dunstan the iconoclast, the destroyer of images. All too often they missed Dunstan the statesman, the architect of what was, for Australia, a genuinely new kind of society. People talk about the '60s as the decade of liberalisation, but in Australia most of the '60s didn't happen till the '70s. What was widely seen as the pivotal cultural event – the hippy musical *Hair* – was performed in Sydney in 1969. The rise of women's lib as a political force took another couple of years, and the gay movement was later still. Although Aborigines had been recognised by the referendum of 1967, the push for land rights was in its infancy. Censorship was rife: police routinely attended the opening of exhibitions and performances viewed as suspect. Multiculturalism was not even a word, let alone a social reality.

And yet in a few short years, Dunstan, as premier of a minor and traditionally extremely stuffy state, turned things upside down. Suddenly South Australia was the pacesetter for social change in Australia, a centre for the arts and artists and, perhaps more importantly, something of a sanctuary for those fleeing the less tolerant regimes to the east. Adelaide, traditionally the City of Churches, became known, only half-jokingly, as the Athens of the South. And in the middle of it all was Dunstan, supported by a kind of republican guard of young Turks, who vied with each other in the old sport of *épater la bourgeoisie*.

In rapid succession, age-old laws against homosexuality were repealed and new ones prohibiting discrimination enacted in their place. Repressive drinking laws were abolished and censorship lifted. Consumer protection was introduced. Capital punishment was abolished. Land rights legislation was drawn up. It all sounds simple and obvious enough now, but at the time it was little short of revolutionary, especially in a state which had always taken itself very, very seriously – South Australia, as the inhabitants never tire of telling you, was the only colony not tainted by a convict past. It had a history of conservatism, even wowserism. Suddenly it seemed to have turned into a continuous festival at which the premier compered Saint-Saëns' *Carnival of the Animals* through a megaphone.

No wonder the establishment hated him. It took a kind of revenge in a particularly ugly bout of rumour-mongering. It was alleged that there was a touch of the tarbrush somewhere in his Fijian inheritance. His sexuality was questioned. Even the fact that he had attended Adelaide's poshest private school, St Peter's, was held against him; it was alleged that dreadful things had occurred during his time there which had since been covered up by nameless forces. When he married his second wife, Adele Koh, the establishment shook its collective head and took the stories to still more preposterous heights.

None of this appeared to worry Dunstan unduly; he responded by appointing Australia's first female judge and first Aboriginal governor, thus further outraging his enemies. He could afford to; his grip on power never really wavered. It remains one of the mysteries of Australian politics how an intellectual aesthete whose principal interests were cooking, gardening and the arts in their more refined forms was able to command such respect and affection from the electorate.

Perhaps the key was his lack of affectation. Dunstan never pretended to be other than he was. Equally, he never talked down to his less well-educated audience; he took them into his confidence in a way few politicians have managed. As a result, they trusted him. And in a perverse sort of way, they took pride in his eccentricities and the notoriety they brought.

Certainly, when grief over his wife's death caused his premature retirement from politics in 1979, there was a genuine sympathy and sadness among the electorate at large. In another politician such a breakdown might have been dismissed as a sign of weakness, an indication that the man was not really up to the job. In Dunstan's case, the distress was so obviously unfeigned that there was only sympathy.

From outside parliament he continued to campaign for social justice with the same passion he had always shown as a politician, but the glory years of reform were over. As in the other Athens, they had been all too brief, but they marked a golden age whose impact is still being felt.

Others have sought to tame Australia, to make it secure, stable and rich. Don Dunstan sought to civilise it. It's not a bad epitaph.

GRAHAM FREUDENBERG

RAHAM FREUDENBERG IS UNDOUBTEDLY AUSTRALIA'S best-known speech-writer, which isn't saying much since probably 99.9 per cent of the population have never heard of him. But they should have.

Freudy is the man who put the Caw in Calwell, the Wit in Whitlam, the Rasp in Wran, the Aargh in Hawke, the Crow in Carr and the Uh in Unsworth (you can't win them all). He is, arguably, the most important Labor insider of the last forty years. He has been at the core of the federal and New South Wales parties; he wrote the definitive history of the Whitlam years (*A Certain Grandeur*), and is the official historian for the state branch.

But until recently he consciously eschewed the limelight, and even when he published his memoir, *A Figure of Speech*, it revealed little about the man himself; at best, it placed him in his historical and political context. As he points out, the role of a speechwriter is to stay in the background, and even in his own memoir much of the private man remains private.

This is a pity, because as those who have worked and played with him know, Freudy could be much more than a figure of speech: he could be a towering presence, whether striding imperiously around the office, scattering ash as he dictated another ringing oration to one of his long-suffering amanuenses, a Beethoven symphony blaring in the background, or holding forth after midnight in the bar, enthralling the faithful with his plaudits for the true believers and his denunciations of backsliders in thunderous and scatological terms, scaring the living daylights out of casual passers-by in the process.

The man we see in the memoir is more observer than participant, but this in itself is dramatic enough: from 1963, when Arthur Calwell almost accidentally took him on as a press secretary, until his contribution to Mark Latham's policy speech of 2004, Freudy has seldom been far from the action.

And his commitment has always been full-hearted. Although brought up as a conservative, he converted at an early age and, like many converts, became more zealous than his mentors. A love of words propelled him into journalism, which in turn gave him his contact with politics; the rest, as they say, is oratory.

He only made one attempt to become a real politician himself, putting himself forward as a candidate for the New South Wales Legislative Council in 1991; he was gracelessly rejected by the heavies of Sussex Street, who nominated instead the corrupt powerbroker Eddie Obeid. But this was late in his career, and the bid was at least partly quixotic. By then he had already contributed more to the party than any backbencher, and than most ministers.

Freudy understood the art of speech: the rhythms, the cadences, the highs and lows. He was also hugely knowledgeable about his topic; behind the verbal sizzle there was always plenty of hard political sausage. But his real genius lay in his ability to get into the minds of the politicians for whom he wrote. He was more than the passionate and persuasive voice of his masters; he was practically their doppelganger.

I first met him during his Whitlam days, and was astonished at their similarity; not only did Freudy use Whitlam's words, but he had his accent, his tone, all his mannerisms. He never really lost them – Whitlam was his first and greatest political love – but later I noticed shades of Neville Wran, another of his heroes, creeping into his speech after he moved to Macquarie Street.

His loyalty and his knowledge (he was a ferocious and retentive reader, especially of political history) made him more than just a speechwriter; he was always part of the inner circle of political advisers, to the extent that he was trusted to put out press releases on his own initiative if his employer was unavailable.

Inevitably his convictions and his enthusiasm led to clashes with the more conservative, especially after lunch; there was the celebrated occasion when he crashed a Whitlam press conference to announce that the prime minister had been snowed by the fucking public service (he promptly offered his resignation, which was of course not accepted). But mostly he kept his own performances for the bar, where they were eagerly anticipated by his numerous friends.

Freudy personifies a time when politics was more boisterous and exuberant; he would be out of place in the Canberra of today, and he knows it, but he is optimistic that the good times will return, as he has always been. One of my lasting memories of Freudy is of waiting with him, a touch tired and emotional, to collect our luggage at Sydney airport. He gestured extravagantly to make a point and tumbled backwards onto the carousel. Aghast, I watched him disappear through the wall, only to emerge triumphantly from the other door, lounging comfortably among the suitcases, cigarette still burning.

They don't make them like that anymore.

MARGARET WHITLAM

Traditionally, the wives of Australian Prime Ministers are expected to be seen regularly supporting their husbands, but heard seldom, if ever. They are certainly not entitled to lives and careers of their own, at least not while they are playing hostess at the Lodge.

Some have been considered better at it than others; Dame Pattie Menzies was of course the doyenne, and by and large those who followed have tried to emulate her example. Even Thérèse Rein, a hugely successful businesswoman in her own right, generally remained in the background while her husband, Kevin Rudd, strutted the stage.

In the aftermath some have blossomed: Zara Holt and Sonia McMahon both enjoyed the social limelight, and Hazel Hawke, after she was dumped by Bob for his biographer, rightly became a national living treasure. But few, if any, have played the upfront role assumed by Margaret Whitlam: she was not just Gough's spouse and helpmeet, she was his partner in every sense of the word, never afraid to disagree with him but always at his side when needed. She too became a living national treasure, and few have deserved the accolade more.

From her early days as the daughter of the Supreme Court judge Bill Dovey, Margaret dedicated her life to helping others. She did a degree in social services and also became a champion swimmer, representing Australia at what were then the British Empire Games in Sydney in 1938. She had ambitions to act but her height – 188 centimetres – proved an impossible handicap. However, it made her the perfect match for Gough Whitlam, 194 centimetres tall, whom she met at the Sydney University Dramatic Society Christmas party of 1939.

'He was just the most divine-looking man I'd ever seen, he had this beautiful dry wit – and he was tall,' she recalled later. Whitlam had acquired a bit of a reputation around town as a ladies' man, if not a pants man; the previous year he had created some frissons as the constant companion of Giulia Bustabo, the visiting American concert violinist. But after he met Margaret, the two became inseparable, and stayed that way for some seventy years. They were married just before Gough was called up by the air force in 1942. After he was discharged, they built a house in Cronulla.

But when Gough won the western suburbs seat of Werriwa in 1951, the family, which by then included four children, moved to Cabramatta, where they were to remain for almost thirty years. It was a bit of a culture shock: no library, hospital or public swimming pool; little transport; no paving, guttering or sewerage. Margaret threw herself into community work and in 1964 became the sole social worker at Parramatta Hospital.

She left her job when Gough became leader of the party in 1967 to spend more time with him in politics. This involved making a new career in the media, with a column in *Woman's Day* and frequent radio and television appearances. Reading Germaine Greer's *The Female Eunuch* confirmed her feminism, and she became a campaigner for equal pay and abortion law reform. Perhaps most importantly, she stayed close to Gough, frequently travelling with him on election campaigns. Her funny, warm and down-to-earth appearances were greatly appreciated by audiences, and particularly by the accompanying press corps, who became devoted fans.

She continued her media career after Gough won the 1972 election, deliberately courting controversy; 'I was never going to just float round opening and closing things,' she told the press. She wanted a proper job, and in 1974 Gough appointed her to the board of Commonwealth Hostels. There was a predictable backlash about nepotism and jobs for the girls, which Gough tried to laugh off: 'She's good in bed and good on the board,' he quipped in one of his less successful jokes. By now the jokes were turning against the pair. Gough continued to take her with him on his overseas trips, prompting the crack: 'He needs her because she's the only woman who can push-start a Boeing 707.'

But on the whole Margaret retained the affection of the public even when Gough was losing it. She was more outraged by the dismissal than he was, and told him he should have torn up the document Sir John Kerr gave him and thrown it back in the governor-general's face; she never forgave either Kerr or Malcolm Fraser, even after Gough achieved a form of reconciliation with the latter. Eventually she put the anger behind her and went on to become an English teacher to migrants, an energetic patron of the arts and finally a tour leader, conducting overseas trips and often taking Gough as her resident historian in a reversal of their previous roles. The two were a fixture on the Sydney arts scene until age finally forced them to curtail their activities.

Margaret used to boast, 'When the Australian people elected Gough, they got two for the price of one,' and few would have disagreed. One of her final honours came at the 2007 federal conference of the Australian Labor Party, when she and Gough were made the party's first two life members. Presenting the award, the president, John Faulkner, commented that Margaret Whitlam had been an inspiration to women across the nation. I felt the need to corner her afterwards and assure her that quite a few of us blokes also thought she was a bit of all right.

Family footnote: in 1975 the Whitlams' eldest son, Anthony, was elected to the federal parliament as the member for Grayndler. Sons frequently succeeded their fathers in parliament, and in one case a father succeeded his son, but only once before had a father and son sat in the House of Representatives together. Not quite another first for the Whitlam clan, but a noteworthy achievement nonetheless.

THE OTHER MOB

ROBERT MENZIES

ON BECOMING LABOR'S FIRST PRIME MINISTER IN TWENTY-three years, one of the first things Gough Whit-lam did was to write to Labor's arch-enemy – the man who had kept his party out of office for most of those twenty-three, Sir Robert Gordon Menzies.

It was a courteous, even flattering letter: Whitlam said that Menzies might be surprised to learn how much the Labor leader had always admired him, not only for his mastery of parliament and politics, but also for his resilience in coming back from defeat to shape the Liberal Party into a modern and dynamic force. This, said Whitlam, was an example he had always held in front of him during his own long battles within the ALP.

Regrettably, Menzies's reply was terse and dismissive: the Labor Party advocated socialist policies, which were wrong for Australia, always had been and always would be, and that was all that needed to be said. He could, perhaps, have been more gracious: Whitlam's compliments were sincere. But by then Menzies had long passed the need for any advice, whether it was praise or censure. His record spoke for itself.

On Australia Day 1966, Menzies had retired as prime minister of Australia. It was his second coming to the post; this time he had held it for sixteen years, one month and eight days, a record unlikely ever to be broken.

In the process he had seen off one opposition leader (Ben Chifley), destroyed another (Bert Evatt) and crippled a third (Arthur Calwell). He had effortlessly eliminated potential rivals in his own party, such as Percy Spender, Richard Casey and Garfield Barwick.

He had amassed innumerable honours, the most prestigious being Knight of the Thistle; in retirement he was to add the even quainter title of Warden of the Cinque Ports. He had acquired two Australian nicknames: Ming the Merciless and Pig Iron Bob.

No wonder his passing seemed to mark the end of an era, an impression enhanced by the relative insignificance of his successors. Within less than seven years, the Liberal Party Menzies founded had been through three leaders and was back in opposition after nearly a quarter of a century of uninterrupted power.

Menzies was indeed the stuff of which myths were made, and the mythmakers went to work with a will. I met the great man just once, when, as a neophyte reporter, I was sent to interview him on the eve of one of his overseas trips. I found him superficially courteous, but underlying it there was an unmistakable air of patronising dismissal. Years later, he said to the American president Richard Nixon: 'In all my life I have treated the press with marked contempt and remarkable success.' Nixon commented: 'I learned a lot from him.'

And of course, it wasn't just the press; his colleagues also suffered. He once told the Country Party's Archie Cameron: 'Cameron, I do not suffer fools gladly.' To which Cameron replied: 'It might be news to you that bloody fools have a lot of trouble putting up with you too.' But few were feisty enough to take the great man on. He was able to play the benevolent autocrat in a way few other leaders have mastered.

Fifty years later, there is a tendency to look back at the Menzies years as a kind of demi-paradise, a carefree, crime-free Australia in which there was no such thing as unemployment or inflation, in which the dream of home ownership was indeed within the grasp of all, in which women, Aborigines and non-English migrants knew their place and were grateful for their share of the apparently endless bounty.

Although he seldom said so explicitly, this was the image John Howard sought to evoke in his many speeches on the national identity: a return to the long summer afternoon, in which a benign father figure effortlessly took the worries of ordinary people on his own broad shoulders.

It is a seductive image, made more plausible by the fact that a majority of living Australians do not remember the period at all, and those who do frequently see it through the rose-coloured glasses the mythmakers have provided. It takes a jolt of real history to demonstrate just how false the image actually is.

The year 1965 was the last full one of Menzies' rule, and was perhaps a livelier one than most; but there is no reason to suppose it was exceptional in what it reveals about the ethics and attitudes of the government Menzies headed. These had been shaped by the Cold War years and by an increasingly cynical exploitation of the fear of communism – more specifically, Asian communism. It had proved a highly successful political tactic: by 1965 the idea of the great continent of Asia looming threateningly over a weak and vulnerable Australia, the red hordes drawn relentlessly southwards by the force of gravity, was a widespread, if hazy, part of the Australian consciousness.

The immediate threat was believed to be Indonesia, under the erratic leftist Sukarno; although the United States was already heavily committed in Vietnam, it was still seen as something of a sideshow. The decision to beef up Australia's involvement was a deliberate attempt to try and lock Washington in to Australia's defence, in case the Indonesian threat got serious.

And indeed Sukarno appeared to have Menzies spooked. Perhaps this was a result of Menzies' previous humiliation at the hands of other non-Anglo leaders, such as Egypt's Nasser and India's Nehru. In addition to the Vietnam caper, Menzies allowed Britain to use Australia as a base for a nuclear strike force, and he went ahead with Australia's own nuclear program, keeping open the possibility of nuclear weapons development to repel an Indonesian invasion (this despite the fact that Sukarno had only the barest outline of a fleet or an air force).

Much was made of the secrecy surrounding Paul Keating's treaty with Jakarta in 1995. Menzies' preparations for war were equally secret and far more frightening.

It is now obvious that few of Menzies' senior ministers and advisers ever believed that Vietnam posed any problems for Australia, or that the 'fall' of Vietnam to communism would precipitate the collapse of the other dominoes of South-East Asia. Fewer still believed that we were pursuing some noble democratic ideal; Canberra's real attitude to foreign democracy was shown when Ian Smith tore up the constitution of Southern Rhodesia and declared unilateral independence. Menzies' instinct was to wish him good luck. It was only after it was pointed out to him that he was in danger of isolating Australia from every country on earth except South Africa and possibly Portugal that he agreed to the British proposal of economic sanctions.

Australia's involvement in Vietnam was based purely on self-interest, which was fair enough, even if the self-interest turned out to be misguided. What is harder to stomach is the deliberate program of lies and deceit that was used to sell it. Anyone who believes that today's politicians are more cynical and less honest than those of fifty years ago need go back no further than the revelations of 1995, when the cabinet documents around that great program of deception were made public.

Still, the idea of a superior morality was part of the Menzies myth, as was the assertion that life under Ming was somehow better than it is today. On most economic indicators it wasn't, even for those comfortably off. But it was certainly simpler.

The White Australia Policy, though tottering, was still in place. Aborigines were yet to be counted in the census, let alone start agitating for real political rights. Strict censorship kept both D. H. Lawrence's *Lady Chatterley's Lover* and Rudyard Kipling's *Barrack-Room Ballads* out of the country. Women in the workforce were rare and discouraged, and there was no suggestion that those who defied popular opinion should receive equal pay. Intellect was suspect, dissent was denounced as communism, and persistent rebels were hounded and denigrated by the security forces, official and unofficial. And over it all presided the great white father, surrounded by his diligent mythmakers. All was right with the world.

Today's supporters of Menzies, if they are honest, will admit that their idol was perhaps not quite the perfect statesman he was cracked up to be; indeed, perhaps he was just a very clever, very ruthless and very lucky politician. However, Ming's people have one unanswerable fallback. 'But,' they will say triumphantly, 'he was such a beautiful speaker.'

It is the one aspect of the Menzies myth that Labor will never be able to emulate or destroy.

HAROLD HOLT

SOME POLITICIANS ARE JUST UNLUCKY. HAROLD HOLT SPENT thirty-one years in parliament before achieving greatness; for the last ten of them at least, he was the heir apparent, waiting patiently for the indestructible Menzies to retire. For seventeen years he had watched the great man see off the easybeats of the Labor Party in election after election: the unstable Bert Evatt three times, and then an Arthur Calwell well past his prime twice more. And when, finally, Holt succeeded to the prime ministership, he was confronted with someone else entirely: the finest parliamentarian of his generation, Gough Whitlam. It just wasn't fair.

It started promisingly enough. In 1966 the ageing Calwell lined up for a last attempt and ran a campaign based on opposition to Australia's participation in the war in Vietnam. At this stage the war was still a popular cause and was made more so when Holt persuaded the American president Lyndon Johnson to make a pre-election appearance on his behalf. Holt and Johnson had hit it off during Holt's

'All-the-way-with-LBJ' trip to Washington, which was derided as sycophancy by the left (on Holt's return, a protestor dressed in scuba gear greeted him with a placard that read 'Frogman does the Australian Crawl') but applauded by the majority.

The protestors were out again during Johnson's visit; when they interrupted his motorcade, the Liberal premier of New South Wales, Bob Askin, ordered his driver to 'Ride over the bastards', to which Johnson rejoined: 'You're a man after my own heart.' But it went well enough to secure Holt a record majority at the polls, finally putting an end to Calwell's ambitions.

And there was another win: with the enthusiastic bipartisan support of Labor, Holt submitted a referendum to recognise Aboriginal Australians in the census and give the Commonwealth the power to legislate on their behalf. It secured an astonishing 92 per cent of the popular vote, a margin never achieved or even dreamt about in any referendum before or since.

But that was as good as it got. Soon after, the Holt government became mired in scandal. The maverick Liberal Edward St John demanded and eventually was granted a second Royal Commission into the fatal 1964 collision between the aircraft carrier *Melbourne* and the cruiser *Voyager*, which showed the government's handling of the issue to have been badly flawed; Holt, having been the navy minister at the time, copped a lot of the flak. Then Holt, on the advice of his hapless minister for air, Peter Howson, misled parliament about the existence of passenger manifests on RAAF VIP flights; eventually the situation was retrieved by the Senate leader, John Gorton, an incident which brought him to the notice of the party's powerbrokers.

But the real problem was Whitlam. Succeeding Calwell at the beginning of 1967, he quickly and effortlessly established supremacy over Holt in parliament, demoralising government forces already debilitated by the retirement of the invincible Menzies. It got to the stage where Holt would complain to colleagues that Whitlam cheated: no sooner had Holt managed to grasp the point of a debate than the wily opposition leader would change the subject. By the end of 1967 an influential section of the Liberal Party, both inside and outside parliament, had concluded that Holt was simply not up to the job; change was needed. A clique led by the ambitious Malcolm Fraser began openly lobbying for a switch to John Gorton.

These manoeuvrings prompted unkind stories that Holt's disappearance in the surf at Cheviot Beach on the Mornington Peninsula just before Christmas was in fact suicide. An even sillier rumour, promulgated by the British journalist Anthony Grey, was that Holt had been abducted by a Chinese submarine. The truth was more prosaic: Holt, along with his wife, Zara, were members of the Portsea set, a party crowd noted for its casual morals. (Zara had three sons from her first marriage, which ended in divorce; Holt legally adopted the three boys, but was later revealed to have been the biological father of two of them.) Holt, a lifelong playboy, embraced the scene with enthusiasm. He had been one of a group which, after an all-night party, had gone to the beach to see the British yachtsman Alec Rose sail into the bay. Also in the group was Holt's mistress, Marjorie Gillespie. The likelihood was that Holt, a skilful but sometimes reckless swimmer, was simply showing off his prowess, with fatal consequences.

In 2005 a belated coronial inquiry found that the cause of Holt's death was accidental drowning. But Holt's political fate had already been sealed. He had been marked by his colleagues for destruction – the first Liberal leader to fall to Gough Whitlam.

JOHN GORTON

OHN GREY GORTON WAS MADE PRIME MINISTER OF Australia for just one reason: to cut Gough Whitlam down to size. The apparently irresistible rise of the new opposition leader was changing the face of politics; having been in power for almost twenty years, the conservatives had come to consider themselves the permanent government of the country; their rule was part of the natural order of things. And yet suddenly, for no good reason that anyone in the Melbourne Club could discern, it was threatened by a bumptious upstart, one of their own who had gone over to the dark side – a class traitor. Clearly something had to be done.

The problem was finding someone to do it. After all those years of unquestioned dominance by one man, the Liberal ranks were seriously depleted. Menzies had disposed of anyone he saw as a possible rival – Casey, Spender and Barwick were long gone. The heir apparent, Harold Holt, had been tried and failed. His nearest competitor, Paul Hasluck, showed little stomach for the fight. Allen Fairhall had withdrawn entirely, David Fairbairn was clearly not up to it, and William McMahon had been vetoed by their Coalition partner, the Country Party led by John McEwen – to the secret relief of many Liberals, who neither liked nor trusted Holt's deputy themselves.

Thus, the lower house was basically bereft of candidates, which left Gorton as their last and only hope. On paper, it was a good hope. Not only was he a proven performer on Whitlam's own grounds – in the parliament and on television, a newfangled medium which most of the Tories were still struggling to master, but Gorton also had a priceless quality that Whitlam lacked. He was instantly likeable – a man of the people, a knockabout chap who could charm the socks off a man or the pants off a woman. He had to be worth a try.

The problem, as quickly became clear, was that few of his colleagues actually knew much about him. He had, after all, spent his entire political career immured in the Senate, which, whatever airs it chose to give itself, was not quite the real thing. The hard stuff, the bare-knuckle fighting, took place in the House of Representatives. Had Gorton lounged for too long in the comfort of the upper house to make the transition? If people had their doubts, few voiced them at the time. The little that was known of Gorton was overwhelmingly positive.

Menzies had made him wait a long time for promotion – a fact in itself that should have given the cautious pause. But once in the ministry, he had performed capably in a series of junior portfolios before entering cabinet as minister for education and science. In 1967 he had become the government leader in the Senate and had rescued the government from the fiasco of the VIP flights kerfuffle. So what was not to like?

Well, as it turned out, Gorton's impetuosity, his reluctance to take political advice, and his impatience with many of the great conservative icons, which he saw as little more than shibboleths and sacred cows. Within a few months of assuming the leadership, Gorton was in open conflict with the conservative premiers, the formidable Liberal duo of Bolte in Victoria and Askin in New South Wales, with the Queensland maverick National Joh Bjelke-Petersen thrown in for good measure. He alienated the DLP, on whose preferences the Coalition depended to retain power, and outraged the traditionalists by replacing the longstanding head of the prime minister's department, John Bunting, with his own ally from the education department, Lennox Hewitt. Worse still, he appointed a pretty and sassy young woman, Ainsley Gotto, as his chief of staff.

And his out-of-hours personal behaviour was less than discreet; he drank heavily and often publicly, paid a long visit to Liza Minnelli's dressing room, and escorted a young female journalist to a party at the American embassy.

None of this deterred his faithful followers, the young Turks of the Mushroom Club. And the public, by and large, thought it all great fun; during a demonstration in support of a unionist jailed for failing to obey a court order, students carried a banner bearing the slogan 'Cut Off Gorton's Penal Power'.

The staid Liberal powerbrokers were first worried, then appalled, but they would have forgiven him if he had delivered what they wanted: Whitlam's political head on a platter. But he didn't; after initial bemusement, Whitlam got on top of Gorton in parliament and stayed there, ridiculing his frequently convoluted speech patterns and cleverly outflanking him on policy. In the 1969 election Whitlam was merciless, quoting Gorton's more labyrinthine utterances to wildly appreciative audiences. When Gorton tried to hit back by attacking the opposition leader, Whitlam responded: 'I'm rather disappointed in the prime minister; I thought we had an agreement that if he didn't tell lies about me, I wouldn't tell the truth about him.' When the election produced an unprecedented swing of 7 per cent against the government, it was clear that Gorton could not last; if he was not replaced, Whitlam and his growing contingent of media backers (of whom I was one) would simply laugh him out of office.

Gorton survived an initial challenge from McMahon, who was no longer subject to the McEwen veto; but when Gorton's erstwhile backer, Malcolm Fraser, precipitated a second challenge by resigning from cabinet, Gorton could only manage a tie in the party room and voluntarily stepped aside. Even then, in a somewhat insane rush of sentimentality, his colleagues re-elected him as deputy leader, a position he held until McMahon managed to sack him for disloyalty. He sat out the decline and fall of the McMahon government as a backbencher, his office a frequent venue for malcontents to drink to McMahon's discomfiture; I was an enthusiastic participant.

Despite our differences, Gorton and I always got on; he remained impossible to dislike. At first he christened me 'The Pard' ('Bearded like the pard' – Shakespeare); later, as my satires became more persistent, I became Mungo Mac-Calumny, but he never held a grudge. And although I remained a dedicated Whitlamite, I always admired his willingness to push through the barriers erected by his own party; there was an element of Whitlam's own 'Crash through or crash' in the Gorton approach.

In the end, of course, he crashed, unable to fight off Whitlam's onslaught from the left or the undermining of his conservative colleagues from the right. But he left more of a mark than did either Holt before him or McMahon after. In racing parlance, he was definitely not the worst.

BILLY McMAHON

W HEN ASKED BY THE BRITISH INTERVIEWER DAVID FROST what was the quality of Billy McMahon that he most admired, Whitlam barely hesitated before replying decisively, 'His persistence.'

A cynic might have added that there wasn't much else to admire, but Whitlam was quite sincere in acknowledging that, whatever McMahon's other failings, he was never a quitter. For many years he pursued the top job through setbacks and humiliations that would have discouraged all but the most determined.

The problem was that while he certainly had the thirst to become prime minister, he had few of the other requisite qualities. A small, prematurely balding man with huge ears, a high voice and a somewhat effeminate manner, McMahon was always treated with suspicion by his colleagues. They found something slightly indecent about his single-minded ambition, particularly when his ceaseless quest for self-promotion crossed the accepted boundaries.

McMahon used regularly to leak details of party room meetings and later cabinet discussions to his contacts on the Sydney *Daily Telegraph*, which was owned by his backer Sir Frank Packer; Packer used openly to refer to him as 'our man in Canberra'. In his diaries Paul Hasluck called McMahon a 'treacherous little bastard'; other colleagues simply gave him the nickname of 'Billy the Leak'.

But they could not deny his lawyer's ability to master a portfolio or to bluff his way though tricky political situations. He boasted of his phenomenal memory, but in fact this was a myth; when answering questions in parliament he would drag numbers out of the air, while his staff, listening to the proceedings in his office, would locate the correct figures and substitute them in the Hansard record before it went to press. The bluff worked for years, and McMahon earned a reputation as an assiduous and competent administrator from the time Menzies promoted him to the ministry in 1951.

Through sheer perseverance, he fought his way up through the ranks, entering cabinet as minister for labour and national service and succeeding Harold Holt as treasurer and deputy leader when Holt replaced Menzies in 1966. It was in this role that his long-held difference with the Country Party leader and deputy prime minister, Sir John McEwen, became an active vendetta; the ostensible cause was McMahon's embrace of free-trade principles to thwart McEwen's protectionism, but the reality was that the two men were polar opposites in every way. Conflict was inevitable.

When Holt died in 1967, McMahon saw the prime ministership as his by right, but McEwen forestalled him by having himself sworn in as a stopgap before declaring that McMahon was unacceptable to the Country Party. Not altogether unwillingly, the Liberals gave way, and McMahon remained their deputy leader, actively plotting against the new prime mister, John Gorton. He enlisted every ally he could find; even I, through my mockery of Gorton's mannerisms and speech habits, was included in the network. Anyone who had ever held a grudge against the prime minister, or who could be persuaded to hold a grudge, received phone calls about the need for change. And when his tireless plotting finally bore fruit and the Liberals discarded Gorton in 1971, I was one of those who thought Whitlam's rise might finally be checked by the new and indefatigable prime minister.

I was wrong, of course; McMahon very quickly became an object of even more ridicule than his predecessor had been. Assailed by an ascendant opposition on one side and a large and vengeful group of Gorton supporters on the other, McMahon retreated to the seclusion of his office to surround himself with paperwork.

In the event, the result of the 1972 'It's Time' poll was a foregone conclusion; needing only a small additional swing to complete the work of 1969, the Whitlam forces could have coasted in. Instead, they ran a largely satirical campaign lampooning their opponent, which was complemented by a far more brutal attack on the hapless McMahon from the combined forces of the Murdoch press. McMahon fought to the end, but the electorate no longer took him seriously. The killer blow was probably the admonition, delivered via a lapel badge: 'Stop laughing at Billy.' The last obstacle to the Whitlam ascension was blown away in a gust of good humour.

BILLY SNEDDEN

GOUGH WHITLAM DID NOT HAVE MUCH LUCK AS PRIME minster; quite apart from the oil price shocks that comprehensively destabilised his government, he had a somewhat unruly parliament to contend with, with both the opposition and his own side constantly creating crises. But he had one initial stroke of good fortune: after 1972, the Liberals made Billy Mackie Snedden their leader. For more than two years, Whitlam found him very comfortable to sit on.

The first time Snedden stood for the leadership of the Liberal Party, he was seen as something of a joke: he was not even in the cabinet, and his mother's accolade – 'He's my baby and I'm proud of him' – did not help. Nor did his claim that he was on the wavelength of his era. In 1968, that was not what the Liberal hierarchy wanted to hear.

But by 1972 they had run out of alternatives. Snedden had advanced to the position of deputy leader under the defeated McMahon and had become the obvious replacement while

146

the Liberals began their regeneration. His record was not a bad one; after three failed attempts he had finally made it into parliament in 1954 and was catapulted into the ministry in 1963 as Menzies' attorney-general, succeeding Garfield Barwick, whom Menzies had pushed aside. When Holt took over he made Snedden minister for immigration, and in 1969 Gorton promoted him to labour and national service. McMahon made him treasurer.

Snedden had ambition, diligence, loyalty and perseverance in his favour, but the big mark against him was that he came from the wrong side of the fence. With his Western Australian working-class background, he would, in theory at least, have been more at home in the Labor Party. He never completely overcame a sense of inferiority in the presence of those who considered themselves his betters, and often made no secret of their belief. His time as leader was beset by those who considered him too moderate, too insecure or just too weak for the job. The DLP leader Vince Gair derided him as someone who was unable to make an impression on a soft cushion or go two rounds with a revolving door.

To compensate, Snedden often went completely over the top in pushing his case. In his leadership campaign of 1968, during which he received just two votes – his own and that of his promoter, Don Chipp – he compared himself to Pitt the Younger, John F. Kennedy and Lee Kuan Yew. Later he described peaceful anti-Vietnam demonstrators as 'political bikies pack-raping democracy'. When his leadership was under challenge in 1975, he claimed that his party would follow him over hot coals through the valley of death. In fact, by that stage quite a lot of them would not have followed him into a pub that served free beer.

His fate was sealed during a debate in which, as Whitlam was reaching his climax, the opposition leader inexplicable interjected, 'Woof, woof.' The silence that followed was broken only by the rustle of Malcolm Fraser adding names to his list of supporters. The outburst confirmed the view of many Liberals that Snedden's hold on the top job should only be a temporary one, a prophecy which became self-fulfilling after Snedden lost the 1974 election, a campaign which he opened with the typically unfortunate observation: 'Wherever I go in Australia, people know that something is wrong.'

In spite of this and other gaffes, he ran Whitlam a surprisingly close race in 1974, indicating that the destabilisation of the Labor government was already well under way. He had laid a foundation on which Fraser could build.

When the Coalition regained office, Fraser shifted Snedden aside by making him speaker, an office of wealth and prestige but no real power. Snedden enjoyed the ceremonial trappings, and filled the role with some distinction and considerable impartiality – an impartiality which often had Fraser gritting his teeth. He also suggested several worthwhile reforms to the workings of parliament and the office of speaker, regrettably few of which were taken up by the government of the day, or any government since.

As speaker, Snedden gained a respect and dignity he had never enjoyed as leader. It was largely lost in the indignity of his death, when his body was found in a Kings Cross motel room, naked except for a condom. But at least, as the Melbourne *Truth* put it in a memorable front page, Snedden died on the job.

MALCOLM FRASER

TWENTY YEARS AFTER HE LOST POWER IN THE FEDERAL election of 1983, Malcolm Fraser was asked by a young interviewer how he thought history would remember his time in government. The ageing but still impressive figure drew himself to his full height. 'Well,' he said, with more than a touch of his old arrogance, 'a great deal better than the Liberal Party does.'

It was a telling riposte. By 2003 the Liberals, turned neo-conservative under Fraser's one-time protégé John Howard, regarded the Fraser years as at best wasted and at worst as something close to treasonous. The belief in treachery was compounded by Fraser's frequent attacks on Howard's policies, particularly his treatment of refugees and his involvement in the invasion of Iraq. And unforgivably, Fraser frequently made common cause against the Coalition with his old antagonist, Gough Whitlam.

Many Liberals would have liked to write him out of their history altogether. Since this was impossible, they took every opportunity to denigrate him in his absence and to snub him if he chanced to cross their paths. Of the ten leaders of the modern Liberal Party, perhaps only the ludicrous Billy McMahon and the ephemeral John Hewson (another critic of Howard) were held in less regard. Even Fraser's great enemy John Gorton, long derided as a figure of fun, was restored to the Liberal pantheon from which Fraser had been exiled.

And yet, while the party that had once hailed him as its saviour now ostracised him, his standing with the general public had never been higher. Since leaving parliament, the aloof Western Districts squatter had remade himself as a classic small-l liberal: a humanitarian, a zealous opponent of economic rationalism, a vigorous and emotional champion of the underdog. His efforts on behalf of international aid through Care Australia – an organisation for which his daughter Phoebe also worked – had earned him the respect and admiration of those who had previously seen him as the personification of uncaring haughtiness, a façade which drew comparisons with an Easter Island statue.

It would be too much to say that he had become loved – his prickly personality precluded that kind of intimacy. But even those who had been his most passionate detractors during his time in politics raised no objection when the erstwhile Squire of Nareen was included in a list of Australia's living treasures.

On one level it was an extraordinary transformation; the beast had suddenly become a prince among men, without even the intervention of a maiden's kiss. But a closer look at history reveals that there were always two Malcolm Frasers. One was the moody, spoiled rich kid with an unquestioning belief in his own righteousness and an unscrupulous determination to put it into practice. But there was another, more complex character as well: a lonely and driven individual with an acute sense of social justice that transcended class, creed and, most particularly, race.

From time to time the two could coexist, albeit somewhat uncomfortably. But usually one has been dominant, and the one we saw during Fraser's spectacular, acrimonious and hugely divisive twenty-seven years in parliament was almost invariably the first.

John Malcolm Fraser was elected to the division of Wannon as the youngest member of the House of Representatives in 1956, following the Labor split that bequeathed the Coalition another ten years of government. After a privileged but isolated childhood on the family property, he was educated at Melbourne Grammar, one of Australia's most expensive and exclusive establishment schools, and then at Magdalen College, Oxford, where one of his tutors remembered him as 'a colonial drongo'. When he entered parliament at the age of twenty-six, he had never had a job.

Even within the Liberals, then a much more class-based party than now, this was not a promising start, and Robert Menzies left the impatient young neophyte on the back bench until his retirement in 1966. Fraser spent his time cultivating those who might prove useful to him, especially fellow social conservatives within the Country Party; it was in this period that he became close to Doug Anthony, Ian

Sinclair and Peter Nixon, the formidable troika who were to become his personal enforcers during his period as prime minister.

Through his continuing acquaintance with B. A. Santamaria, the sinister nemesis of the ALP, he also made useful contacts within the Democratic Labor Party, the predominantly Roman Catholic rump which had split from the main body and was now dedicated to keeping Labor out of office at all costs. It is interesting that he apparently felt more at ease with the two right-wing fringe groups than he did with his own mainstream Liberals.

He also developed his own philosophical stand; he became an avid fan of Ayn Rand, the ultra-rightist American, which confirmed his own prejudices against any form of collectivism, especially as practised in the trade union movement. (Interestingly, Rand herself, when asked for her views during a visit to Australia, was unsure of the depth of Fraser's commitment: 'I don't think he's quite selfish enough,' she said percipiently.) But his attempts to become one of the boys at the members' bar invariably fell flat; he simply lacked the social touch. His idea of a joke, which was to slip pickled onions into the coat pockets of his fellow drinkers, probably didn't help either.

Harold Holt finally plucked Fraser from the back bench and installed him in the portfolio of army – which, while in keeping with Fraser's increasing interest in defence, was not nearly senior enough for the ambitious Victorian, who was now worried that rivals from his own generation such as Billy Snedden, Peter Howson and Don Chipp – and even newcomers like Andrew Peacock and Phillip Lynch – might be stealing a march on him. As Holt began to falter against the opposition Whitlam in 1967, Fraser repaid his patronage by becoming a leading figure in the conspiracy to have him dumped, preferably in favour of one of Fraser's few genuine allies in the party, John Gorton.

In the normal course of events the plot would probably have come to a head in the first half of 1968; as it happened, Holt was drowned at Cheviot Beach before the conspirators could act, and the battle for succession replaced that for replacement. Once Gorton was installed, he promptly rewarded his supporters; he gave Fraser the ministry of education, and after the 1969 election promoted him to defence. But before long the two men started to fall out.

Unlike many of his more straitlaced colleagues, Fraser was not overly concerned about Gorton's drinking and womanising, but he was worried by his style of one-man-band government; in particular, he didn't like what he saw as interference in his own portfolio. In July 1970 there was a serious clash over whether, and if so how, the Pacific Island regiment should be called out in the event of rioting in Papua New Guinea; the disagreement was apparently resolved, but Fraser was to make much of it in his resignation speech nine months later.

Gorton and McMahon, now minister for foreign affairs, continued to veto some of Fraser's more ambitious ideas, and the relationship reached breaking point. In March 1971 a dispute over plans for civic action in Vietnam provided the trigger. With the enthusiastic aid of the New South Wales press, led by McMahon's patron, Sir Frank Packer, Fraser pulled it. His resignation precipitated the downfall of Gorton and the ascension of McMahon, who nonetheless failed to invite the hangman to the victory feast; Fraser remained on the back bench for five months before being restored to his old portfolio of education, which he held until the Coalition finally lost office in 1972.

In opposition under Billy Snedden, Fraser was given the non-job of primary industry spokesman; his full-time job, however, was to undermine his leader. At his own expense he engaged a public relations firm to improve his image; it failed to convince most of his colleagues, especially the moderates, now led by Andrew Peacock. But with Whitlam effortlessly demolishing Snedden in parliament, although his inexperienced government was clearly cracking under both economic and personal stress, Fraser established himself as the tough alternative – the only one who had Whitlam's measure. Fraser pretended to remain detached from the campaign to overthrow Snedden, a sham that fooled no one, but by the start of 1975 a majority of Liberals were desperate enough to overcome their dislike and distrust of him. It had taken nearly twenty years, but he finally assumed the leadership for which he had always believed he was destined.

The Labor government was by now in such disarray that Fraser could have simply waited for power to fall into his hands at the next election. Once again, however, impatience got the better of him. Having repeatedly denied any intention to use his numbers in the Senate (which had been acquired through unprecedented breaches of convention by the conservative premiers of New South Wales and Queensland) to block supply, he proceeded to do so after what he described as 'extraordinary and reprehensible circumstances'. Faced with a similar position in 1974, Whitlam had gone straight to an election; this time he held out.

Throughout the crisis that followed, Fraser appeared perfectly confident; almost alone among the seething masses in Parliament House, he believed Whitlam's own governor-general, Sir John Kerr, would end the dispute in his favour. Whether this was foreknowledge or simply amazing prescience, 11 November proved him right. Kerr sacked the government and installed Fraser as prime minister, enabling him to win the subsequent election in a landslide. His first biographer, John Edwards, wrote at the time: 'No Australian Prime Minister came to power in such extraordinary circumstances, after such a perilous career, with so few friends, so many enemies or so large a majority, as Malcolm Fraser.'

Given this style of ascension, it might have been supposed that Fraser would have unleashed a conservative revolution; indeed, in his wide-ranging speeches of the previous year, he had given notice of nation-shaking changes, and as leader of the first government in twenty years to have control of both houses he was in an unrivalled position to bring them about.

But to the relief of those already reeling from three years of seismic change, including many in his own party, the Fraser regime was largely uneventful. Critics from both sides of politics suggested that, deep down, Fraser himself knew that his grab for power was tainted. But even after he won another thumping majority in 1977, the pace did not quicken. There were desultory attempts to dismantle some of the more radical changes Whitlam had made, although many were left intact; and there were a series of occasionally ugly confrontations with the trade unions, although nothing permanent was achieved.

On the whole, it was a time of recovery, though definitely not of reconciliation. For nearly half the population Fraser remained a devilish figure, and few of the rest gave him more than grudging respect. He even managed to alienate his right-wing supporters: to their bewilderment and fury, he supported Aboriginal land rights, took on the racist regimes of South Africa and Southern Rhodesia, opened the door to Vietnamese refugees and forced the Queensland government to end sand mining on Fraser Island, presaging the other Malcolm Fraser who would emerge after retirement.

He was tough on his ministers, sacking even confidants such as Reg Withers, who had delivered him the numbers in the Senate, for what others saw as trivial offences – perhaps another attempt to establish his political legitimacy. In the end he was reduced to a core of genuine supporters, mainly from the Country Party. Few mourned when the absurdly popular Bob Hawke knocked him off in 1983.

He was, of course, famous for saying: 'Life wasn't meant to be easy.' He later justified this gloomy conclusion by paraphrasing the full quotation from *Back to Methuselah* by George Bernard Shaw: 'Life wasn't meant to be easy, but take courage, child – it can be glorious.' But while there was great excitement and some success in Fraser's life, it is hard to point to much that was glorious. It is more likely that his secret credo was summed up in an interview at the height of his prime ministership:

Q: Rightly or wrongly, the 'life wasn't meant to be easy' tag has been attached to you.

A: Well, it isn't, is it?

Perhaps therein lay the real Malcolm Fraser.

DOUG ANTHONY

I WAS EASY TO UNDERESTIMATE DOUG ANTHONY, AND MANY people did – to their cost. The clear, direct gaze, the boyish curl of blond hair, the smiling mouth that always looked as though it should be chewing a blade of grass – Anthony looked like the archetypal country boy, even the country hick.

But behind the disarming façade, there lurked a shrewd and resolute political mind. In hindsight, it should have been obvious: you did not get to the top of the party of Earle Page, Artie Fadden and Black Jack McEwen by being an amiable yokel.

John Douglas Anthony entered the parliament in 1957, one year before Gough Whitlam. He inherited the northern NSW seat of Richmond following the sudden death of his father, Larry, who had been postmaster general and minister for aviation in the Menzies government. When he retired in 1984, there was a twelve-year pause before Richmond was won by his son, Larry Junior, who in turn held it for eight years, making the Anthonys the only three-generation political dynasty in Australian history. Between them, they held Richmond as their personal fiefdom for fifty-five of its first 103 years.

And it did not happen by chance. From the time young Doug, as he was always known, completed his education at the Sydney King's School and Gatton Agricultural College, his father was grooming him for the job. In the same year he entered parliament he married Margot Budd, a member of a local family which owned the local newspaper and had a share in the radio station. When television arrived in the district, the Budds took an interest in that as well. During those early years, Anthony seldom had to worry about unfavourable treatment in the media.

In 1964 he was given the traditional Country Party testing ground of the interior ministry, but then in 1967 he took the important post of minister for primary industry. It was thought that even then McEwen was preparing him to take over the leadership, but he had a rival in the ambitious Sydney solicitor Ian Sinclair. In the end Anthony's superior rural background prevailed and he became the Country Party's sixth leader since its formation in 1920, just in time for the change of government in 1972.

From the start, there was tension with the Liberals. In opposition the formal coalition was dissolved, but Anthony, as a party leader, still insisted that he held precedence over the Liberal deputy leader, Phillip Lynch. The actual opposition leader, Billy Snedden, watched helplessly as the two men jostled each other for the position of second-most important man in opposition. Eventually, Anthony resolved the impasse by squatting in the deputy's office and refusing to move. And he immediately asserted his newly acquired clout by insisting that the opposition parties take a tough line against the Labor government – no concessions, no quarter, and the interlopers were to be forced out of office as soon as possible.

His concern was a valid one; for the Liberals, the Whitlam regime might be an ideological aberration, but for the Country Party, it posed an existential threat. Whitlam was a passionate believer in a policy of one vote, one value; he was determined to abolish the system by which rural seats were given a population allowance, meaning that their parliamentary representatives – usually the Country Party – had to service far fewer constituents than their city counterparts. This gerrymander was justified by demography – some of the rural electorates were vast, and took literally weeks to cover, while the city seats fitted into a comfortable day's travel.

But Whitlam was determined to change it, and Anthony saw that the change could significantly reduce his party's parliamentary numbers and even put it on the road to oblivion. Thus, when in 1974 Whitlam hatched his plot to bribe the DLP senator Vince Gair to leave the Senate and thus give him the numbers to force his reforms through, Anthony took swift and decisive action (as described below).

Whitlam, thwarted, called a double-dissolution election, as a result of which the DLP was eliminated from parliament altogether, but he did not win his Senate majority. During the election campaign, Snedden and Anthony clashed repeatedly, particularly over Snedden's plan for a wage-price freeze;

Anthony said his party could not and would not support what he called a 'cheap food' policy. After the election Anthony effectively abandoned Snedden to throw in his lot with Malcolm Fraser; their shared rural background made the two natural partners. And in 1975 Anthony became the second-most important man not in opposition, but in government: deputy prime minister.

Whitlam continued to mock his mispronunciations – 'mischievous' and 'grandiose' were special problems – but he could hardly deny that the hayseed had emerged a winner. Anthony took the mantle of greatness lightly; when Fraser was out of the country and he became acting prime minister, he frequently oversaw the nation from a caravan parked on his holiday block at New Brighton beach. He and his fellow Nationals (as the Country Party had now been renamed) Sinclair and Peter Nixon became a loyal and sometimes feared praetorian guard around Fraser, and Anthony became Fraser's chief confidant and enforcer. But he had no taste for another stint in opposition; he retired soon after the government fell at the end of 1983 and went back to the farm, staying out of politics except to support his son, who needed it; Larry did not inherit his father's political nous.

I had always found Doug a congenial sort of bloke while in Canberra, and when I moved to the Northern Rivers in 1988 we renewed our acquaintance. Anthony was by no means a hard-line right-winger, having voted to decriminalise homosexuality in the ACT, and he later became a quiet but dedicated supporter of the republican cause. I also got on well with Margot, an accomplished pianist.

There is a curious story associated with this: during the 1980s a trio of students formed an anarchic comedy troupe which they called, for reasons which are not entirely clear, the Doug Anthony All Stars. Margot, unfazed, rechristened her chamber music group the Margot Anthony All Stars. She was astonished to receive a call one day from a man claiming to be the Doug Anthony All Stars' manager, railing at her for ripping off his band's name. 'If it hadn't been for us, no one would ever have heard of Doug Anthony,' the man spluttered.

Well, perhaps he did not become a political superstar. But those who knew him remembered him, all right. Just ask Gough Whitlam.

ANDREW PEACOCK

THERE ARE POLITICIANS WHO SEEM DESTINED TO BECOME prime minister and there are others who you just know will never make it. They are seldom the same person, but Andrew Sharp Peacock was the exception. He was not so much the Liberals' golden boy as their gilded boy.

His career started out as a dream run. The son of a wealthy company director and the product of the finest education money could buy, he became president of the Victorian branch of the Liberal Party at the age of twenty-six. Just a year later he inherited the finest piece of electoral real-estate in the nation: the division of Kooyong, held by the great Sir Robert Menzies for almost thirty years. He breezed into Canberra in the autumn of 1966 and became John Gorton's minister for the army in 1968. His youth and freshness made him a popular figure, even among his opponents; in the Liberal Party of the day he was a moderate, even a progressive.

When Billy McMahon switched his portfolio to territories, Peacock made common cause with Gough Whitlam in rejecting the conservative approach of Paul Hasluck towards Papua New Guinea, which involved glacial progress towards independence at some unspecified date in the distant future: Peacock and Whitlam instituted a program of rapid change and development, which led to full independence for the colony in 1975.

But in spite of his obvious ability, some of the longer-serving Liberals had their doubts about their enthusiastic young colleague; things came to him too easily, and perhaps he lacked the toughness and commitment that the long haul in politics demanded. They called him 'the Show Pony', pretty to look at but not suited to real work. And Peacock was indeed a vain man; he insisted on being photographed in left profile, which he thought was his handsome side, and sported a permanent artificial suntan, which earned him another nickname, 'the Sunlamp Kid'. In later years Paul Keating accused him of dyeing his hair and dismissed him with the devastating line: 'A soufflé does not rise twice.'

His film-star good looks made Peacock a natural ladies' man. His first marriage was to Susan Rossiter, the daughter of a Victorian state minister, and the highly visible couple became known in social circles, unkindly, as 'Soupy Cock' and 'Droopy Cock'. Susan left him for richer pastures and Peacock became a sole parent to their three daughters, but continued to seek the company of women through numerous affairs. The most public of them was with the American actress Shirley Maclaine, a member of the notorious

Hollywood rat pack along with Frank Sinatra, Dean Martin and Sammy Davis Junior. She christened Peacock 'the foreign minister from central casting' and proclaimed, 'I'll give him a foreign affair.' Later she said he was the only man she had ever met who owned a Gucci toothbrush. In 1983 Peacock married another long-time mistress, Margaret Wright, but the affair with Maclaine continued at every opportunity and his marriage did not last. He married for a third time while serving as ambassador in Washington.

When the Coalition went into opposition in 1972, Peacock became a senior figure on the front bench, and after Snedden lost the 1974 election he was spoken of as a possible leadership contender, if only to stall the unpopular Malcolm Fraser. But the more ruthless and ambitious Fraser made all the running, and in the end Peacock's only role was to force the final showdown. In government, Fraser rewarded him with the prestigious foreign affairs portfolio, but there were always tensions between the two, especially over policy regarding Cambodia. After the 1980 election Peacock switched to industrial relations, and a year later brought on a challenge to Fraser's leadership, using terms identical to those used by Fraser against John Gorton in 1971. But unlike Fraser, he was unsuccessful, and he went to the back bench until Fraser forgave him and recalled him to the front bench in 1982, effectively endorsing him as his chosen successor over Peacock's main rival, John Howard.

Back in opposition, Peacock and Howard played musical chairs with the leadership for the next seven years, in the course of which they lost three elections between them, two with Peacock as leader. After the 1990 defeat he retired from politics, leaving the field to Howard. When Howard won government in 1996, he made Peacock Australia's ambassador to Washington, a job which recognised that his real talent lay in the rituals of international diplomacy rather than the roughhouse of Australian politics.

Before leaving Australia, Peacock tacitly acknowledged that he had spent most of his life in the wrong game. Asked whether he still wanted to become prime minister one day, he replied meekly: 'I'm not sure that I ever did.' It was not an admission Gough Whitlam could ever have made; indeed, such a wimpish lack of drive would have been incomprehensible to any truly ambitious politician. But then, one of the more attractive things about Andrew Peacock was always that he wasn't really one.

JAMES KILLEN

CROSS-PARTY FRIENDSHIPS IN POLITICS ARE NOT AS RARE as is commonly thought; thrown together in the hothouse of parliament, many political enemies find they have much in common that transcends the often minor differences debated with such passion on the floor of the house. And few have formed a closer bond than Gough Whitlam and that other great character of the parliaments of the '60s and '70s, Sir James Killen.

The two men were united by a love of words and language, by a zest for obscure classical allusions, and above all by a respect amounting to devotion to the parliament and all its rituals. They both had their setbacks and failures, but they never lost their faith in the system on which both made an indelible mark.

The passing of Denis James Killen in 2007 marked the end of not one political era, but two. Even in his heyday the man was something of an anachronism – a throwback to an earlier and more flamboyant age when style and oratory ruled the parliament, when political debates were won and lost on the floor of the chamber rather than in the opinion polls, and when the overriding ethos was one of camaraderie rather than malice.

He played the part to perfection, always impeccably turned out in a well-tailored suit complete with weskit and watch-chain, more often than not finished with a red carnation as a boutonniere. His dark hair was sleekly oiled and his moustache impeccably trimmed. His fruity and orotund sentences flowed without hesitation and, it must be admitted, sometimes without much logical consistency; his vocabulary often exceeded his grasp of semantics. But he could always command an audience.

During his twenty-eight years as member for Moreton, Jim Killen (even after his knighthood he was seldom known as anything but plain Jim) made many friends and few enemies, delighted both colleagues and foes and was always a favourite of the press gallery. But while his success on a personal level was unmatched, the same could not be said of his political career. Indeed, there must have been times when he wished he had stuck to his other great loves: the law and the racetrack.

Like a surprising number of Liberals of his generation, Killen came from a humble background. He was born in rural Queensland and as a teenager worked as a jackeroo. In later years, when he was accused of racism over his hardline support of white rule in southern Africa, Killen answered his critics with the devastating line: 'Mr Speaker, I can surely claim to be the only member of this house who has swum bare-arsed in the Condamine with Aborigines.' Requests for photographs of this historic event were, however, refused.

Like Whitlam, Killen served in the RAAF during the war and entered parliament in 1955. But unlike Whitlam, he failed to advance through the ranks. Sir Robert Menzies found his views too extreme and his style too theatrical.

He might have hoped for better when, in the cliff-hanger election of 1961, Moreton was the last seat decided, and a handful of Communist Party preferences saved the government. Not realising that the preference flow was actually a result of the donkey vote (the communist candidate headed the ballot paper and Killen's name appeared above his Labor rival's), his colleagues hailed Killen as a miracle worker, but he waited in vain for acknowledgement from his leader. Eventually, after prolonged hounding by the press, Killen invented a telegram from Menzies: 'Killen, you are magnificent.'

Ming the Merciless was not amused, and Killen had to wait another seven long years for Menzies' retirement before he was admitted to the ministry. At least the wait gave him time to gain extra qualifications as a practitioner of law and a student of horseflesh.

Salvation came with the accession of John Grey Gorton, another knockabout character who had much in common with his protégé. Killen was given the junior department of navy, into which he threw himself with a somewhat reckless zeal. In his memoirs he recalled ruefully:

> During my first visit to HMAS *Melbourne*, while being shown over the engine room I spoke with a

stoker. I was dressed in overalls and we exchanged names. 'And what do you do?' he asked. 'Well,' I replied, 'as a matter of fact I happen to be the minister.' Without batting an eyelid he looked at me and said, 'Smart bastard!' It was one of the kindest things ever said about me and there were many times when I wished the summation had been correct.

The ministry failed to restrain Killen's natural exuberance. Together with some other new ministers, including Andrew Peacock, Don Chipp and Tom Hughes, he formed a dinner group which they christened the Mushroom Club, on the grounds that they were kept in the dark and fed bullshit. Typically, when Gorton heard of it he insisted on joining; he was given a special tie and the title Chief Spore. But when Gorton was deposed in 1971, Killen and Hughes were both dropped from the ministry by Billy McMahon, and the club dissolved.

Both took their sackings very hard. Killen had a particular dislike for his replacement, the unctuous Malcolm Mackay, a contempt shared by Whitlam. The two conspired in a parliamentary exchange in which Whitlam asked Mackay a question that, he said, his predecessor had been considering. Could Mackay take up the issue? Killen interjected: 'But is he of the same calibre?' to which Whitlam responded: 'He is of a lesser calibre, but is a bigger bore.'

Unlike Hughes, who left politics to become one of Australia's highest-paid lawyers, Killen hung on as a baleful presence on the back bench. He compared his large-eared prime minister to a Volkswagen with both doors open and bagged him mercilessly to anyone who would listen. At one party meeting, McMahon was haranguing his troops about how hard he worked on their behalf and declared dramatically: 'I sometimes think that I am my own worst enemy.' Killen replied with deep conviction: 'Not while I'm alive.'

He was returned to the front bench for the Coalition's three years in opposition during the Whitlam years, a time in which he and Whitlam briefly suspended their practice of sending each other notes with classical references across the chamber. And when Malcolm Fraser took power in 1975, Killen was rewarded – to the surprise of many – with the plum defence portfolio, making him one of the government's most senior ministers.

He held the job for nearly seven years, though not without controversy; at one stage he told parliament, and through it a startled electorate, that the military forces were so run-down that they would have trouble defending Bondi Beach on a sunny Sunday afternoon. His remedy was to set up the Australian Defence Force Academy, his lasting political monument. When Fraser was finally ready to move him on, Killen was offered his pick of diplomatic postings, but family problems and the death of a daughter prevented him from leaving.

Then Fraser retired after losing the 1983 election and Killen's old friend Andrew Peacock left him out of the shadow ministry. Killen retired from parliament shortly afterwards, but kept himself in the public eye with writing and speaking engagements and, in 1998, a quixotic attempt to return to parliament. Perhaps fortunately, he failed. It is hard to imagine that the colourful, gregarious and sometimes outrageous extrovert would have found a niche among the grey apparatchiks who dominate the parties today.

Killen will be remembered with affection, and perhaps a tinge of regret that his full potential as a politician was never really put to the test. In an increasingly tough profession, he generally preferred to be a bit of a dilettante – a gentleman rather than a player. He lived in a period when speechifying was the essence of politics, and that was where he devoted his talents. Jim Killen was not as fluent as Menzies, as forensic as Whitlam, as erudite as John Wheeldon, as passionate as Eddie Ward or as funny as Fred Daly. But no one was better at looking and sounding like the very model of a parliamentarian.

At his best he was a vigorous and committed advocate for the process he loved. And he was never less than a distinguished ornament to it. At his funeral it was left to his old friend and sparring partner Whitlam to reprise his self-awarded accolade of 1961: 'Killen, you were magnificent.'

BILL WENTWORTH

WHEN I MOVED TO CANBERRA IN 1969, IT WAS LIKE migrating to another country; the language and customs were utterly different from those of the Australia I knew, and the people themselves seemed something of an alien race. But when I finally brought myself to enter the old but still imposing edifice of Parliament House, there was one familiar, if not always friendly, face to greet me: Uncle Bill.

Bill Wentworth was my mother's brother and had been a frequent visitor to his own mother's Point Piper residence, where I spent much of my childhood. A noisy and often abrasive presence, he nonetheless was treated with all the indulgence he demanded as the eldest son and heir. He had little time for children, including his own, but for some reason picked me as being bright enough to receive some of his accumulated wisdom, which he delivered in diatribes of which I seldom understood a single word.

Nonetheless, he was always stimulating company and I

had followed his political career with some interest, including his long-awaited appointment to the ministry; after a frustratingly long time on the back bench, his friend John Gorton had finally given him the dual portfolio of social services and Aboriginal affairs. Alas, it did not last; after what must have seemed like the blink of an eye, Billy McMahon relegated him to the back bench once more.

I felt it my nephewly duty to visit his office to commiserate. I could offer nothing but the inane line, 'Things could be worse.' Uncle Bill fixed me with his customary steely glare. 'And they will be,' he snapped. And from his point of view, of course, they were; the advent of a Labor government was the last straw. The socialists, nay, the commos themselves, had finally gained power.

William Charles Wentworth IV came from a long line of politicians, the first of whom was independent, eccentric, opinionated and ferocious in dispute. In many ways the ancestor was recreated in the descendant.

But in one respect the later Wentworth was never quite able to reach the heights to which his generous talents entitled him. Australian politics after the Second World War was more formal, more institutionalised, more respectable than it had been in the rambunctious nineteenth century. In the long shadow of Menzies, Wentworth's ambitions failed to flower. In twenty-eight years as a member of the House of Representatives, he served in the ministry for a bare three. And yet few of his contemporaries made such an impact or left such a legacy.

As the eldest son of a proud, if sometimes unconventional, family, Wentworth was automatically named after his famous forebear and brought up in wealthy environs and high expectations. He was educated at the prestigious Armidale School and then at Oxford, where he excelled academically. On his return he became an adviser to the New South Wales Treasury under the Liberal government that succeeded the stormy administration of Jack Lang. It was during this period that his views on the necessity of government regulation of the economy hardened. He remained a dedicated opponent of the *laissez-faire* approach and its successor, the so-called 'economic rationalism', all his life.

In the war years he became a captain in the army reserve, and severely annoyed his superiors by taking the exercises seriously. On one famous occasion he simulated an invasion from Cronulla Beach, captured the local battalion headquarters and arrested the colonel in his pyjamas. While such exploits pointed up the unreadiness of Australia's defences, they added to Wentworth's reputation for hotheadedness and instability. His political views also tended to the extreme; he embraced what has been described as 'the catastrophic view of history', and his virulent anti-communism, even by the standards of the time, was sometimes embarrassing to his colleagues.

He was a founding member of Menzies' revamped Liberal Party and entered parliament when it took government in 1949. He had high and justifiable hopes of advancement, but in fact Menzies was never to promote him. Refusing to stagnate on the back bench, he threw himself into committee work. He became the driving force behind standardising the rail gauge between Sydney and Melbourne; nonetheless, when the new line opened, he was not invited to the ceremony.

His indefatigable wife, Barbara, appeared on the platform instead, bearing a placard demanding, 'Where's Wentworth?' Its publication in several papers made the point.

There was to be a curious echo of such pettiness many years later, on the anniversary of another of Wentworth's great achievements: the referendum to include Aborigines in the census and thus make it possible for the federal government to legislate on their behalf. Wentworth had persuaded Menzies to agree to the poll, which was finally held under Harold Holt in 1967. It was a seminal moment in Australian history, yet Wentworth was again left out when the Labor government celebrated the twenty-fifth anniversary in 1992.

In other fields he was less successful. His diatribes against the communist menace inspired more hilarity than fear in his opponents; on one occasion, Labor's Les Haylen appeared in the house wearing a borrowed white coat and offered to escort him out. But he persevered with his anti-communism long after it ceased to be fashionable (and before it became fashionable again) and was one of a handful of members who refused to join in a parliamentary tribute on the death of Mao Tse-tung.

Menzies' retirement and the death of Holt finally ended Wentworth's long stay on the back bench. He supported Gorton for the leadership and was rewarded with the dual portfolio, becoming the first federal minister of Aboriginal Affairs, in which cause he had worked so diligently. He threw himself into the work and achieved a lot, not only within his own area. At one budget cabinet meeting he appeared with a massive pile of documents in which he reviewed every aspect of the economy.

But his day was to be short-lived. Bill McMahon ousted Gorton early in 1971 and Wentworth, loyal to Gorton and his centralist approach, was an inevitable casualty. His return to the back bench finally brought his frustrations to the boil. In opposition he pursued Whitlam and his ministers relentlessly, even backing a court action against them. Passed over again when Fraser led the conservatives back to government, he became equally acrimonious against his own side. Eventually he resigned from the party and stood unsuccessfully as an independent senator in 1977. He was to have one last crack at politics seventeen years later, when he stood for the House of Representatives in the seat named after his famous ancestor: 'A Wentworth for Wentworth.'

But while rejection, first by his party and then by the electorate, undoubtedly soured him, it did little to diminish his energy. In retirement as in office, he travelled extensively, camping in the outback more often than using city hotels. He wrote many articles and letters on current issues, usually denouncing the policies of both major parties. His passion for argument lasted until his death.

These days, it is easy to see Wentworth as something of a caricature of the old-style conservative – as a man who, even in his heyday, was already out of his time. But in fact his approach to domestic issues, especially national standards, pension reform and Aboriginal affairs, was ultra-modern, even groundbreaking, in the '50s and '60s.

His tragedy was that too often the extravagance of his

style caused people to overlook the value of his substance. His triumph is that the substance will still be recognised long after the style is forgiven and forgotten. Certainly his old foe Whitlam acknowledged it; he turned up unexpectedly at Wentworth's unpublicised funeral service, a gesture which was greatly appreciated by the family – especially, of course, by me.

DAVID FAIRBAIRN

SIR DAVID ERIC FAIRBAIRN LOOKED, AND FREQUENTLY acted, like a real born-to-rule Tory, the sort Gough Whitlam always detested and sought to destroy. His family was the nearest thing to Australian aristocracy, and while his own manner was courteous and self-deprecating, it was often mistaken for condescension – as, in fact, was Whitlam's own. For this reason alone the two never became enemies; although their politics were poles apart, each genuinely respected the other's integrity.

Fairbairn was perhaps the last of the gentlemen politicians. He came from a family dedicated to public service, and continued the tradition in a world which increasingly failed to appreciate the contributions of aristocratic amateurs like himself. During his career in public life, he saw the standards by which he set great store eroded and eventually changed beyond recognition, but he never wavered in his belief that he had a duty to persevere.

He was not a colourful figure; his school (Geelong Grammar) magazine records that in 1931 he appeared in a Vergilian play-pageant as a Sicilian dressed in gold, green and rose-coloured garments, but such flamboyance was definitely not part of his public persona. The flashiest thing about his parliamentary performances was his tie (Cambridge Hawks).

Nor was he a forceful personality; the real strength and ambition in the Fairbairn family came from his wife, Ruth, of whom it was frequently said that if she had been a man, she would have overthrown Sir Robert Menzies and become prime minister herself. But Fairbairn was a constant force for stability and old-style conservatism within the Liberal Party and successive Australian governments. The word most often used to describe him was 'dependable'.

Fairbairn entered parliament in 1949 after a distinguished military career with both the RAF and the RAAF. It was the election at which Menzies returned to power; for the next twenty-three years Fairbairn was never to sit on the opposition benches, a circumstance which sat easily with his somewhat patrician approach to politics.

However, despite his impeccable background, he remained a fairly unobtrusive backbencher for thirteen years. It was not until 1962, when the Liberal ranks had been severely depleted, that Menzies summoned him to the government as minister for air. In that capacity he oversaw the purchase of the controversial and expensive F-111 fighter bomber, and acquitted himself well enough to be promoted into cabinet as minister for national development in 1964.

His five years in this portfolio covered some interesting ground, including rail standardisation, the completion of the Snowy River scheme, the Ord River scheme, the oil exploration boom and an abortive move towards nuclear power generation. But although Fairbairn enthusiastically took up the ideas of others, he was not an innovator himself. This had clearly suited Menzies, who did not encourage his ministers to adopt a high profile, but after the grand old man's departure in 1966 there was an obvious need for new blood.

Fairbairn took a back seat in the leadership machinations that followed, but when John Gorton took the leadership after the death of Harold Holt, Fairbairn found himself increasingly uncomfortable with the direction in which Gorton was taking the party. The two men both came from rural Victoria, but otherwise they were total opposites. Fairbairn, the urbane gentleman farmer, conservative to his bootstraps, could not approve of Gorton, the dishevelled larrikin orchardist, determined to break away from the shibboleths of the Menzies era.

The eventual confrontation between the two was over the issue of states' rights, but if it had not happened when it did, in 1969, it would have happened sooner or later. Uncharacteristically, Fairbairn found himself in a leadership role, indeed a rebel leadership role. He stood against Gorton, but more as a symbol than a serious contender; the bulk of the anti-Gorton votes went to William McMahon, who finally toppled Gorton eighteen months later. In the meantime, Fairbairn returned to the back bench to head a small but influential bloc of rebels who continued to undermine the prime minister.

McMahon recalled him for a brief stint as minister for education and he later replaced Gorton in defence. When the Coalition finally lost power in 1972 he had his first taste of opposition, did not like it, and retired quietly in 1975. In the Gorton years he had considered applying for a diplomatic post; in 1977 Malcolm Fraser gave him one and he served a term as ambassador to the Netherlands. He returned to Australia in 1980.

In 1988, after a long fight with the bureaucracy, he became a naturalised Australian citizen.

Although the Fairbairns had been Australian for three generations, David was born in England and had conducted his entire public life in Australia as a British citizen. In those casual times, no one had bothered to query the matter. Fairbairn, who had a well-developed and self-deprecating sense of humour, must have been tempted to mention it himself, particularly when Paul Keating launched one of his anti-English diatribes. But, a gentleman to the last, he never did.

PHILLIP LYNCH

T HE MOST SURPRISING THING ABOUT PHILLIP LYNCH WAS HIS
politics. His father was a Melbourne fitter and turner,
his mother a humble housewife, and the family was
staunchly Catholic. His natural home was the Labor
Party, and indeed he nearly became a member while at Melbourne University; he was active in a number of leftish campaigns, notably for the abolition of the White Australia Policy.
But in the end the excesses of Labor's Victorian Left were too
much for him, and he joined the Libs – yet another misfortune
for Gough Whitlam to lay at the door of his ideological foes.

Lynch became a successful management consultant and
was actively involved in a number of employer organisations,
His political career followed a familiar path – he contested a
safe Labor seat, lost it, and was rewarded with a winnable
seat next time around. He entered parliament in the landslide election of 1966, one of a large and ambitious group of
newcomers; as a working-class Catholic, he was considered
the least likely to succeed.

But John Gorton gave him the junior but sensitive ministry of army in 1968, where his name became known as part of an anti-war slogan. The minster for national service, in charge of conscription, was Les Bury; students took to the streets chanting: 'Lynch Bury and Bury Lynch!' It was a tough initiation; Lynch was also involved in an incident in which Australian officers in Vietnam were accused of using water torture to interrogate a female Viet Cong suspect. Lynch dismissed the reports, saying that there was not a scintilla of evidence. When eyewitnesses came forward, he was forced into a humiliating backdown.

He was switched into the immigration portfolio, and under Billy McMahon was promoted to labour and national service. When the Liberals went into opposition, he unexpectedly became deputy leader of the party under Billy Snedden, the first Catholic to hold the position. However, Doug Anthony insisted that he, not Lynch, was the actual deputy leader of the opposition. Lynch supported Snedden until after the 1974 election, but when he saw the way the political tide was running, he switched his allegiance to Malcolm Fraser, an act of betrayal for which Snedden's supporters never forgave him.

As Fraser's shadow treasurer, Lynch was largely responsible for exposing the loans affair. Lynch had an informant in Treasury who fed him a steady stream of information; this man, known at the time as 'Mr Williams', was later named under privilege by Senator Peter Walsh as a deputy secretary, Des Moore. The scandal led to the sacking of two senior ministers, Jim Cairns and Rex Connor, and set up the conditions for Fraser to block supply and force the crisis which led to the dismissal of the government. Lynch, it was felt, had proved his worth.

But as treasurer in Fraser's government, he frequently found himself outgunned by the protectionists in the National Party, with whom Fraser usually sided. He failed to achieve any worthwhile reforms and in 1977 came to grief when the opposition attacked him over his involvement in land dealings in Victoria and the purchase of a unit in Surfers Paradise. Fraser had already called an election. Lynch had gone to hospital, suffering, it was said, from kidney stones, but for Fraser the newspaper cartoons of an invalided Lynch announcing that he was 'a little crook' were insupportable. Lynch was told his resignation as treasurer was accepted whether it was offered or not and the portfolio was given to John Howard.

Even so, Lynch remained the party's elected deputy leader and moved to the ministry of industry and commerce, where he remained until his health gave way in 1982. He died two years later. At his funeral, Labor's polymath Barry Jones eulogised: 'I do not think that those of us who are paying tribute to Sir Phillip Lynch would mark him out as a man of extraordinary intellectual brilliance. He was not. But he was a man who developed the capacities he had by sheer unremitting work. He never gave up ... He could outsit anyone else ... when people were fainting in coils, Sir Phillip Lynch was writing the minutes.'

And in one case, they were minutes that led to the downfall of a government. For an unremarkable man, Lynch achieved at least one spectacular result.

MAGNUS CORMACK

THE SENATE WAS WHITLAM'S GREAT ROADBLOCK, THE OBSTACLE he never overcame in his quest to ram through his ambitious program while time remained. At one stage he lamented to his friend Jim Killen, 'When I die, they will find the word "Senate" engraved on my heart.' And for the impatient prime minister, the obstructiveness of the upper house was personified in two men: his own Senate leader and factional opponent Lionel Murphy, and the Senate president, the imperturbable Tory Sir Magnus Cameron Cormack.

In the late 1960s the two joined forces in a highly unlikely alliance that was to change that august body from a parliamentary retirement home to an important political force. The archetypal rural conservative joined forces with the radical Labor lawyer to upgrade the chamber's moribund committee system and turn it into something like the high-profile inquisitorial network of the United States Senate. Both men had grown impatient with the Senate's seeming irrelevance and comparative anonymity. They were determined to raise the status and prestige of what Sir Magnus always referred to as 'the senior house'.

They succeeded spectacularly, and in the early 1970s the Senate emerged as a new dynamic on the political scene. Sir Magnus himself became the powerful chairman of the Senate Select Committee on Securities and Exchange, which ran an investigation into the many rorts and abuses that characterised the mining boom of the 1960s. Although the committee's work reached its climax under his successor, Peter Rae, it was Sir Magnus who set the pattern for what was to become a completely new role for the upper house.

It was an unusually public role for the western Victorian grazier, who had been a powerbroker within the Liberal Party since his recruitment by Menzies in 1945. He narrowly missed election to the House of Representatives seat of Fawkner in 1949, and then had a short stint in the Senate from 1951–53, before being re-elected in 1962.

In the intervening period Sir Magnus was responsible for enticing John Gorton away from the Country Party to the Liberals, and helped secure him his Senate seat. On the death of Harold Holt in 1967, he was one of the key group of supporters who saw Gorton take over as prime minister – a move he was said to have later regretted.

Certainly it failed to secure him a place in the ministry, which many of his colleagues felt he had earned. Perhaps as a result he became something of a campaigner against what he saw as a dangerous tendency towards unaccountable rule by the executive, and a champion of the more open parliamentary system.

In 1971, partly as a result of the success of his committee work, he was elected as president of the Senate, a role to which he was perfectly suited. It was, unfortunately, a brief climax to his political career; the election of the Whitlam government the following year led to his replacement, and to his retirement from parliament in 1974.

He remained active behind the scenes, however, and was an important member of the group that raised Malcolm Fraser to the party leadership in 1975. The final meeting in which Fraser's supporters plotted the downfall of Billy Snedden was held in Sir Magnus's Toorak flat, thus confirming him as the kingmaker of his time.

But it is as Senate president that he will be remembered. Always urbane and often witty, he ran the chamber in a generally even-handed and avuncular manner which is still held up as a model for his successors. He also appreciated the perks of office, becoming a lavish entertainer in the luxurious presidential suite.

Even in the chamber he had his privileges. In the evenings of long sitting days, an attendant would often approach him, resplendent in wig and gown on the presidential throne, with what appeared to be a tumbler of water. It was an open secret that the drink was in fact a gin and tonic. It is a measure of the regard in which he was held that none of his Senate colleagues ever queried this minor indulgence.

This regard was not always shared by the wider public. And among the press gallery, his pomposity earned him the nickname 'Sir Bogus Throwback'. On one memorable occasion, a group of Aborigines took advantage of a visit by

Queen Elizabeth to protest about the delay of the Whitlam government in introducing land rights legislation. They assembled on the steps of Parliament House, demanding to see the prime minister.

Sir Magnus, as a former presiding officer, took it upon himself to deal with the situation. He informed them politely but firmly that their request could not be granted at that time; the prime minister was in fact having an audience with the Queen. 'Well, fuck the Queen!' responded the leader of the group.

Sir Magnus, a devout royalist, gasped with horror and retreated to the parliamentary bar for a stronger than usual G-and-T. When Whitlam saw the delegation later, he explained to them that unfortunately their suggested course of action would have constituted a severe breach of protocol.

REG WITHERS

R EGINALD GRIEVE WITHERS TENDED TO REMIND THE MORE literate Whitlam supporters of Shakespeare's King Claudius – the one of whom Hamlet said, 'One may smile and smile, and be a villain.'

The Liberal leader in the Senate was unfailingly cheerful and usually grinning, albeit in a sometimes unctuous fashion. One erudite journalist described him as pinguid; I once compared him to an unhygienic butcher who has just palmed off a dodgy pork chop on a pensioner. Even to his own team, his constant smugness was exasperating. But no one, whether friend or enemy, could deny that he delivered the goods.

When he arrived in Canberra in 1968, Withers already had a reputation as a lawyer who took no prisoners, a man with whom it was unwise to tangle. And in spite of his jovial manner, his talents as an enforcer were quickly recognised by his colleagues. Within a year he had been appointed the government's chief whip in the Senate, a job in which he was christened 'The Toecutter' for the ruthless manner in which he maintained party discipline.

When the Coalition went into opposition he became opposition leader in the upper house, determined to use his numbers to force the government out of office as soon as possible. He made no secret of his aim. As early as March 1973 he was dismissing the election result as 'an aberration on the part of a few thousand people living in the outer suburbs of Sydney and Melbourne'. And aberrations were there to be corrected: 'Because of the temporary electoral insanity of the two most populous states, the Senate may well be called upon to protect the national interest by exercising its undoubted constitutional rights and powers.'

Thus, he was keen to block supply at any opportunity. He enthusiastically backed Bill Snedden's move in 1974, and then switched support to Malcolm Fraser, in whom he sensed a far more pitiless and unscrupulous ambition. To Fraser and Withers, what mattered was getting back on the Treasury benches, and they were not going to miss out next time around; in 1975, it was Withers' job to keep his troops together until the crunch came.

It was not a task for a wimp; a handful of senators had grave doubts about the death-or-glory charge Fraser had sent them on, and the worries ranged from the genuinely ethical to the frankly political. One defector would have ended Fraser's grab for power, and probably Fraser and Withers with it. The stakes were very high, but Withers embraced them, and with threats and cajolery held the line until Sir John Kerr dropped his bombshell on 11 November.

Not unnaturally, Withers expected a lavish reward, but in the new government had to make do with the comparatively junior portfolio of administrative services. And even that did not last. In 1978 a Royal Commission found that Withers had acted improperly in regard to an electoral redistribution. By the normal standards of the times, this was hardly a hanging offence, but Fraser, conscious that a large proportion of the electorate still believed that he had gained power illegitimately, was keen to show that his government observed the highest standards. He called Withers in, offered him a cigar and declared: 'The meeting has decided that you must go. I am therefore withdrawing your commission tonight.' Withers replied coolly: 'As you like. Thanks for the cigar.'

Outside the room he was more forthright: 'When the man who's carried the biggest knife in the country for the last ten years starts giving you a lecture about propriety, integrity and the need to resign, then he's either making a sick joke or playing you for a mug.' For the next five years he sat on the back bench, white-anting Fraser at every opportunity; Withers was the principal force behind Andrew Peacock's unsuccessful challenge to Fraser in 1981.

Back in opposition after 1983 he was openly bored, and when John Howard, whom he despised and blamed for his expulsion from the ministry, became leader, enough was enough. He did not contest the 1987 election, and it was said that he would have lost his preselection if he had attempted to. Withers returned to Perth, where he served from 1991 to 1994 as lord mayor, a job perfectly suited to his public style. But he was said to look back with some nostalgia at his glory days as a mover and shaker in Canberra. Or perhaps he just missed the toecutting.

DON CHIPP

D
ON CHIPP WAS AN IDEALISTIC LIBERAL. NOWADAYS, THAT
would be a contradiction in terms; in these unforgiving
times, idealism is not a quality fashionable in Australian politics, and particularly not in the Liberal Party.

The qualities now demanded from a politician are ruth-
lessness single-mindedness, the killer instinct; winners are
interested in results, not ideas. Idealism is best left to the do-
gooders and bleeding hearts; it might rate a ritual mention on
special occasions, but it has nothing to do with *Realpolitik*.

It was not always so. Back in the 1960s there was a faction in the party which was not only moderate in its views
but optimistic, rational and even visionary in its agenda for
social reform, and at the centre of this faction was the young
Donald Leslie Chipp. It was for this reason rather than any
pursuit of political balance that I asked him to join Gough
Whitlam as a godfather (well, mentor, sponsor – whatever
the humanist equivalent is) for my younger daughter when
she was born early in 1973. That, and an obsessive love of

cricket, which we shared – perhaps I hoped that some of it would rub off.

Chipp's record in the ministry was regrettably short: a brief shot at the navy portfolio under Harold Holt, then a period on the back bench before being appointed by John Gorton to customs and excise, which he held until the fall of the McMahon government in 1972. In opposition he shadowed social security, but Malcolm Fraser dumped him after gaining power in 1975 and that was it. In 1977 he resigned to form the Australian Democrats, which he led as a senator from 1978 until he retired from parliament in 1986.

It is for this role that he is now chiefly remembered, but it is worth noting that he remained, at heart, a Liberal: committed to free enterprise, passionate about the rights of the individual and suspicious of the welfare state. As a progressive he was drawn to many aspects of Labor policy and often supported Labor initiatives in the parliament, but he never even considered crossing the line.

The conservatives in the Liberal Party, including his old enemy Fraser, made him out to be a dangerous lefty, but this was always unfair. Chipp was always firmly committed to what another politician described as the extreme centre. It was this that made him so hard to deal with.

And in Liberal terms he was always an outsider; like his friend Billy Snedden, whom he supported for the leadership as early as 1968, he came from a working-class background before studying commerce at the University of Melbourne and eventually winning a senior position in administering the 1956 Olympic Games.

Even then he was a fierce competitor with an eponymous chip on his shoulder; he used to complain about being left out of the university football team because, he maintained, he was not part of the establishment. He was a hard man on the cricket field; in later years he captained the parliament against the press gallery and sledged ferociously – although, it must be said, his politician teammates copped more abuse than his opponents.

He was a good enough athlete to run in the Stawell Gift, and took part in a charity race on the Gold Coast, which he swore he won, although he was adjudged by the then prime minister, Billy McMahon, to have come second. He would never believe that McMahon's decision probably had more to do with myopia than with malice; as always, the establishment was out to get him.

And yet his best friends in parliament were both establishment pillars: the Sydney QC Tom Hughes and the rising Melbourne star Andrew Peacock. Chipp craved acceptance, but was always wary of it.

A similar contradiction was evident in his time in the ministry. No customs minister did more to break down the absurd and outdated censorship laws in Australia, but none was more intransigent on the subject of drugs. Chipp held screenings of movies up for classification for his fellow members, explaining with exemplary patience and courage why he believed the previously unscreenable should be available for adult viewing, but he refused even to listen when the same members suggested that a similar tolerance be extended to occasional consumers of cannabis. There were limits to his commitment to individual freedom.

But once he had embraced a cause, he was unwavering. In 1962, little more than a year after he had won his seat in a by-election, the government introduced a bill providing for capital punishment, to which Chipp was morally opposed. The new boy sought an appointment with Prime Minister Menzies to tell him that he could not vote for it, an act of defiance which a somewhat taken-aback Menzies approved.

This was Chipp the idealist in action: a man of uncompromising honesty, he believed this was the way politics should be conducted. But of course, these *Boy's Own Paper* standards did not apply in the real world, and never have; as a result Chipp was constantly wavering between high principles and deep disillusionment.

A typical example came when Holt, whom Chipp had admired, drowned in 1967. The senior ministers were genuinely shocked and grieved, but being practical men, they also bent their minds to the succession, and their own chances of gaining the top job. To most politicians, this was simply common sense. To Chipp, it was an act of unconscionable bastardry. Yet his own enthusiastic, if utterly quixotic, support for his friend Billy Snedden ('a man on the wavelength of his generation') was apparently quite okay – decency was more a matter of timing than consistency.

Although initially snubbed for the ministry by Gorton, Chipp later became a wholehearted supporter of the new prime minister. In the reshuffle following Gorton's narrow win in the 1969 election, Chipp was given customs and excise. When McMahon ousted Gorton in 1971, Chipp, unlike his friends (and fellow Mushroom Club founders)

Tom Hughes and Jim Killen, retained his job, but he never forgave McMahon for what he saw as his disloyalty to Gorton (those principles again).

He was, of course, even more unhappy about Malcolm Fraser, whose calculated resignation had triggered Gorton's downfall. In opposition he fought as hard as possible to prevent Fraser from gaining the leadership, but was nonetheless outraged when he was left out of Fraser's ministry.

After a year brooding about what he saw as Fraser's autocratic style, Chipp wrote to tell him so. In due course Fraser summoned him to deny the charge, and ordered Tony Street, one of his more acquiescent ministers, to tell Chipp that he, Fraser, did not dominate cabinet. Street dutifully did so. Chipp records: 'I burst out laughing, but neither Fraser nor Street could understand why. I remember thinking: what's the bloody use!'

By this time, Chipp was making numerous speeches outside parliament, often on the same platform as those whom the Libs under Fraser regarded as the enemy. These included members of the Australia Party, a child of the Liberal Reform Movement, which had been born in 1967 from Liberals opposed to the war in Vietnam. Initially a supporter of Australia's role, Chipp now regarded it as a mistake; he was attracted by the idea that there could be a genuine third force in Australian politics, but reluctant to take the leading role.

However, when he finally resigned from the Liberal Party in March 1977, he was simply swept up by a popular wave of support. He had never been more than a junior minister; suddenly he was a political star. Within two months the

Democrats were a reality; within seven they were fighting an election. And 'they' really meant Chipp, the party's public face; becoming more frazzled as the frantic weeks passed, he was christened by one journalist 'the sincere prune'.

The party was in fact an extension of the man: the slogan 'Keep the bastards honest' said it all. The Democrats were founded on an idealism the professionals pronounced unworkable: no real socio-economic base, no overall national structure, and no genuine party discipline: they were, their critics proclaimed, the fairies at the bottom of the garden. But they survived and even flourished; in 1986 Chipp handed over to Janine Haines a party which, if not yet a genuine third force, had certainly been a bloody nuisance to Fraser and his successors.

In later years Chipp saw the Democrats lose their way and eventually fulfil the critics' predictions. But he never lost his optimism or his belief that idealism was the only real basis for politics in a civil society. To the end, he played the game as he played his cricket: determined to win but always within the rules, and always true to the spirit of the code as he saw it.

He would not have been embarrassed by the old epitaph: 'For when the One Great Scorer comes / To write against your name / He marks – not that you won or lost – / But how you played the game.'

PETER HOWSON

EVEN IN DEATH PETER MICHAEL HOWSON HAD IDEAS above his station. In a rather confused obituary in the *Australian*, Caroline Overington described him as Australia's first minister for Aboriginal affairs. Of course he wasn't; that honour belongs to William Charles Wentworth, a committed fighter for the cause who was appointed by John Gorton in 1968. At the time Howson was merely part of a backbench clique undermining Gorton on behalf of William McMahon.

When McMahon finally got the top job in 1971, Howson lined up for his reward; having held down a junior ministry during the Menzies, Holt and even Gorton years, he thought he was in line for promotion. But it was not to be. As he left the new prime minister's office, a colleague asked him what he had got. Howson snarled back: 'The little bastard gave me trees, boongs and poofters.'

He was referring to the admittedly incongruous grab bag of environment, Aborigines and the arts, three areas in which the McMahon government had not the slightest interest. In that sense, Howson was the ideal choice. His ignorance of the environment led me to christen him Peter Howson-Garden. His disdain for matters aesthetic resulted in Phillip Adams describing him as a pain in the arts. And on Aborigines, he was a dedicated Hasluckian: they would assimilate or they would die out, it was up to them.

Howson lost his seat in 1972 and left Canberra unmourned and unmissed, particularly by Gough Whitlam, who saw the English-born upstart as a painful anachronism. But some thirty years later, the culture-history wars saw him resurrected by the right-wing magazine *Quadrant*. Along with another political nonentity of similarly paternalistic views, Labor's Gary Johns, he became one of editor P. P. McGuinness's resident authorities on Indigenous Australians. He outlived his editor and survived to hear Kevin Rudd's long overdue apology to the stolen generations, which he had derided as a silly fairy tale.

He had, Overington informed us, a lifelong commitment to the deaf. That figures.

EDWARD ST JOHN

W HEN EDWARD HENRY ST JOHN, QC, MP, PUBLISHED AN apologia for his political career in 1969, he called it *A Time to Speak*. The reference was to the Book of Ecclesiastes: 'To everything there is a season, and a time to every purpose under the heaven ... A time to keep silence, and a time to speak ...' His colleagues frequently wished that St John had observed more of the former and less of the latter.

Throughout his three years as Liberal member for the safe seat of Warringah, he assumed the role of a Socratic gadfly, constantly stinging the government into action on issues it would much sooner have left alone. For this reason there was never any chance that he would rise above the back bench, but in his brief and stormy time in parliament he attracted more attention than many ministers receive in their entire careers.

The son of a country parson, he saw a move to politics as a natural step in a career that had always been driven by a sense of duty and justice. In many important areas his instincts were more to the progressive side of politics than to the right, but the ALP held no attractions for him. He saw it as too doctrinaire, too rigid in its prescriptions for a better world. And of course, he would have nothing to do with socialism in any form. St John was perhaps the closest thing we have seen in parliament in the postwar era to a genuine old-fashioned Liberal in the English mould: definitely a Whig rather than a Tory. This meant that he had more in common with independently minded thinkers of the left, including Gough Whitlam, than with the majority of his conservative colleagues.

After serving in the AIF he was called to the bar, but he continued a number of outside interests. He was chairman of the Council of Civil Liberties, a member of the Malta Constitutional Commission and a founding member and later president of the Australian Council of the International Commission of Jurists. In 1960 he set up the anti-apartheid body SADAF (South Africa Defence and Aid Fund), which made him some bitter enemies on the far right of the Liberal Party.

These ran a vicious campaign against St John when he stood for Warringah in 1966, a campaign St John thwarted (typically) by taking his detractors to court. He won the seat easily, but found his high-minded expectations of political life dashed by the pragmatic reality of Canberra.

Undeterred, he joined other disgruntled backbenchers in their crusade to reopen an inquiry into the sinking of the HMAS *Voyager*. In a remarkable maiden speech, St John provoked the prime minister, Harold Holt, to the point where he broke tradition by interjecting against the new member. St John paused before replying icily: 'I did not expect to be interrupted by the prime minister.' The crusade infuriated Holt and his navy minister, Don Chipp, but in the end they were forced to hold a second Royal Commission, which reversed some of the earlier findings.

Having got firmly offside with his political peers, St John proceeded to espouse the cause of higher salaries for members of parliament, scarcely a popular cause among the general public. He attacked some aspects of government policy on Papua New Guinea and Rhodesia, and queried the terms of purchase of the F-111 fighter bomber. This last caused the then minister for air, Gordon Freeth, to complain about St John's 'odour of sanctity'. His supporters replied that there were worse things to smell of, but by this time St John had been firmly labelled a maverick and a trouble-maker. Many of his colleagues were deeply offended by his apparent self-righteousness. The fact that he very often genuinely was right only made matters worse.

Things finally came to a head when St John publicly attacked Gorton, newly elected as prime minister, over his behaviour during and after a press gallery dinner, which culminated in a late-night visit to the United States embassy in the company of a young female reporter. St John had been becoming increasingly disturbed at what he saw as the larrikin element in Gorton. From his idealistic – some would say unrealistic – perspective, Australia's prime minister should be above reproach, a model of conduct for the rest of the community. On another level, St John, a firm states' righter, was unhappy about Gorton's centralist approach to government.

Again, he decided it was time to speak – but this time the Liberal establishment had had enough. Mrs Gorton published a poetic parody describing St John as 'the member with the serpent's tongue'. The party room decided it would prefer him not to take further part in its meetings. His electorate, and in particular his old enemies of the right, put pressure on him to resign his Liberal endorsement. He did so, but continued to proselytise through the universities and the alternative media, some of which had motives less pure than his own for attacking Gorton and his government.

Against the advice of his friends, he decided to contest Warringah as an independent at the 1969 election. In a close election there was the bare possibility (horrifying to both the Coalition and the Labor Party) that he could hold the balance of power in a split parliament. But it was not to be, and Warringah returned to the Liberals in the form of the amiable and uncontroversial Michael MacKellar.

St John went back to the law and his other interests, leaving behind a situation which he described apocalyptically as 'the very nadir of our political life'. He would probably be struggling to find words for today's roughhouse. There can be little doubt that he was well out of it. The then defence minister, the modest and acute Allen Fairhall, pronounced St John's political epitaph in 1969: 'He is too independent and too pure of heart.' Again, his supporters might say that there were worse excesses.

So St John's unswerving morality played its own small part in the downfall of Gorton and the McMahon debacle, which led to the fall of the government he had once, briefly, supported. Whitlam had always treated him as a friend; in the end he turned out to be a valuable ally.

MICHAEL HODGMAN

THERE HAVE BEEN MANY MORE ACCOMPLISHED POLITICIANS than Michael Hodgman, but none more enthusiastic. He bounced into Canberra like an untrained puppy in the Liberal landslide of 1975, determined to be noticed and loved, and over twelve long and often frustrating years, never lost his initial fizz.

He had enjoyed a brief apprenticeship in the Tasmanian upper house, but this was scant preparation for national politics. However, he wasted no time in establishing his position among the crowd of new Liberal backbenchers. He was first and foremost a patriotic, flag-waving Tasmanian. Indeed, he commissioned some miniature Tasmanian flags, which he proudly carried with him so that he could be photographed at any opportunity. He developed a stock reply to any criticism from his Labor opponents: 'Mr Speaker, why do they hate Tasmania?' And he never wavered in his support for states' rights and for the monarch, whom he regarded as Queen not of Australia but of Tasmania. Inevitably, he became known as 'the Mouth from the South'. Gough Whitlam, once again the opposition leader, used, in deference to the militant feminists who frequently surrounded him, to refer to the new member as 'Mr Hodgperson'.

His closest friend and ally was his fellow Apple Islander Bruce Goodluck, a less flamboyant character who lived largely in Hodgman's shadow – although he did once appear in the house with sky-blue hair, which he sheepishly attributed to an experiment by his young daughter. Hodgman and Goodluck shared a Canberra flat. This was a common enough practice among the parliamentarians, but Goodluck once felt compelled to justify the arrangement at a public meeting, during which he repeatedly assured his bewildered constituents: 'Michael and I are not homosexuals.'

The news would have come as no surprise to observers in Canberra, where Hodgman had thrown himself into the social whirl, such as it was in those days. A conventionally handsome figure, with dark hair and clear skin (which he ascribed to frequent applications of Vaseline), snappily dressed with his trademark buttonhole, he cut quite a dash. He was a keen party animal, but also a practising Roman Catholic and a fervent supporter of the Right to Life anti-abortion lobby group, whose founder, Margaret Tighe, once described him as her greatest asset. And he was a zealous, almost fanatical, anti-communist; indeed, some of his colleagues felt that he would have sat more comfortably with the DLP than in their own ranks.

But he always did his best to fit in, to the extent of turning out for the politicians' cricket team in their annual match against the press gallery. He was not a success. His über-competitive captain, Don Chipp, finally tossed him the ball with the instruction, 'Well, you can't bat and you can't field, Hodgman, maybe you can bowl.' Alas, he couldn't, and after an over of wides and lollipops he was banished to fine leg.

But then, as always, he cultivated the journalists, probably more indefatigably than any member before or since. His constant appearances in the press gallery became a source both of anticipation and dread: anticipation because in the endless stream of gossip and self-promotion there occasionally appeared the nugget of a story, and dread because he could be almost impossible to get rid of. I once had to physically manhandle him out of the office so that I could get on with my work.

But he was never deterred by rebuffs, at that or any other level. And eventually, in 1980, Malcolm Fraser rewarded him with a junior ministry. The parochial Tasmanian was put in charge of the ACT. He tackled the job with his customary verve. One highlight came when he and a *Canberra Times* reporter, Gay Davidson, discovered an unhappy Canberran about to set himself on fire on the steps of Parliament House, and managed to persuade him not to.

Another involved a resident who was discovered painting his garage with the image of a swastika. A complaint was laid and Hodgman arranged for a Dorothy Dixer to be asked in question time. On cue he leapt to his feet, bellowing, as I wrote at the time, like a maddened thesaurus. This was horrible, terrible, wicked, evil, awful and atrocious and he wouldn't put up with it, he cried; the swastika would go! Just what ordinance he intended to invoke was not clear; it sounded rather as though he was planning to fire-bomb the premises.

Fortunately, it turned out that the painter was not a neo-Nazi, but merely an eccentric who had been experimenting with a series of different designs. He was happy to move on to the next one, which was, from memory, the rising sun of Japan, considered inoffensive. The episode made the local headlines, but even Bruce Goodluck suggested that perhaps Michael had gone a bit too far this time. In any case, the glory was short-lived; in 1983 Labor was back in power and four years later Hodgman lost his seat. After a long break he returned to state politics in 1998, finally retiring in 2010.

He did not survive to see his son Will win the 2014 election and become Tasmanian premier. Will did not divulge whether he planned to take his father's 2007 advice to 'give the Labor Party one right up the bracket'. Even in his political twilight the fire had not gone out of his belly. And Michael Hodgman still needed to be noticed.

VINCE GAIR

THERE IS A STORY THAT WHEN VINCE GAIR ARRIVED IN Canberra as a new senator in 1957, he was spotted in Kings Hall, looking lost and bewildered, by Labor's legendary kingmaker Pat Kennelly. Kennelly, like any Labor man, had been taught to despise the DLP apostate as a deserter who had ratted on his party, but the veteran took pity on his fellow Irishman.

'Son,' he said, 'let me give you some advice. There are two doors that lead out of this hall. The one in the middle leads to the library, and the one on the right leads to the bar. And how well you succeed in this place will depend on which of those doors you choose.'

'Gee, thanks,' replied the grateful Gair, and disappeared immediately through the door on the right, to what quickly became his chosen habitat. But this did not mean that he ignored the library; he could frequently be found there after lunch, ensconced in one the comfortable leather chairs, a newspaper draped across his mottled face, his breathing slow but regular.

Vincent Clare Gair was always treated as a deserter by his former Labor colleagues, but he was never ostracised as completely as were his DLP colleagues from Victoria. They were the cold-blooded traitors, the ideologues and zealots who had been seduced by the arch-demon B. A. Santamaria to the dark side; their sin was irredeemable. But Gair had joined the DLP almost by accident; in Queensland the split was not about dogma but about power, a concept all politicians could contemplate with understanding and even sympathy.

As premier of Queensland in the '50s, Gair had attempted to use the anti-communist industrial groups, precursors of the DLP, to break the power of the two unions that dominated Labor in the sunshine state: the Australian Workers' Union on the right and the Trades and Labour Council on the left. But he succeeded only in uniting them against him. They forced a crisis, used their combined power to expel Gair from the ALP, and then went back to fighting each other. Gair and his supporters then formed the Queensland Labor Party, but the split ensured that the conservatives easily won the next state election, setting up a period in office that lasted from 1957 until the fall of Joh Bjelke-Petersen and his short-lived successors in 1989.

Gair, politically bereft, was enticed by the DLP with the offer of a Senate spot, and grabbed it. In Canberra he found himself confronted by the formidable Victorian Frank McManus, who, with some justification, saw himself as the DLP's natural parliamentary leader. When the pair were joined at the next election by Condon Byrne and Jack Little, however, it was Gair who won the job. With the DLP holding the balance of power in the Senate, he carried immense, if largely undeserved, political clout, and was not afraid to use it. The DLP generally supported the Coalition government – after all, the whole point of its existence was to keep Labor out of office – but was never reluctant to vote with the ALP if it saw an advantage.

It was, of course, fiercely anti-communist, forcing the government as far as possible to the right on defence and foreign affairs. Its other obsessions were state aid for church schools, strict censorship and, in line with Catholic doctrine, opposition to homosexuality, abortion and euthanasia. Beyond these sacrosanct areas it could be flexible, and the DLP required and received constant stroking from both sides of politics.

Perhaps the high point of Gair's power came when Gorton planned an early election in 1968 to consolidate his position; Gair vetoed it, saying that the DLP would run dead, and threatening to withhold the preferences that kept the Coalition in office. It was almost certainly a bluff, but effective as a warning shot; he expected more from the new prime minister than he had yet received.

The two men clashed frequently: once, as Gorton was about to embark on an overseas trip, Gair farewelled him with the admonition, 'Behave yourself.' Gorton wheeled on the senator. 'John Grey Gorton will bloody well behave precisely as John Grey Gorton bloody well decides he wants to behave,' the prime minister snapped.

But Gair was not finished. 'Personally, I couldn't care less if John Grey Gorton jumps into the Yarra and drowns himself,' said the portly senator. 'But John Grey Gorton also happens to be the prime minister of Australia. I do care about how John Grey Gorton conducts himself as prime minister of Australia.'

Gorton was outraged; coming from a man who had been the subject of a formal complaint by Ansett air hostesses (who protested that whenever they were compelled to serve him, they ended up with his fingerprints all over them), this was the sheerest hypocrisy. But there was little Gorton could do about it; he needed the DLP's support in the Senate to govern, and still more he needed DLP preferences come election time, especially in Victoria. Indeed, these were the only thing that saved him in 1969. But by 1972, with the reform of the Victorian ALP and the consequent dilution of the DLP vote in that state, they were no longer enough. Gough Whitlam led Labor to victory and the DLP's *raison d'être* disappeared.

This seemed to have its effect on Gair: he was drinking more and enjoying politics less. He was contemptuous of the new opposition leader, Bill Snedden; Snedden, he loudly informed the members' bar, could not lead a flock of homing pigeons. With the Liberals in opposition, Snedden could afford to hit back; he said he would no longer deal with the DLP if Gair remained leader. McManus pounced and took the leadership he had always believed was rightfully his. Gair let it be known that he would leave parliament when his term expired in 1976.

Which led some smarties in the ALP to ask themselves: why not sooner? Why not at the half-Senate election due in 1974? If Gair left, there would be six, not five, Queensland seats in the mix, and Labor would have a very good chance of picking up the sixth, thus achieving its long-held dream of a Senate majority and a clear passage for the Whitlam program.

The opportunity was too good to pass up; Whitlam himself embraced the plan with enthusiasm, and Gair suddenly found himself surrounded by new drinking mates from his original party. Prominent among them was the Labor leader in the Senate, Lionel Murphy, who appointed himself chief plotter and in March of 1974 delivered Gair to Whitlam's office for an offer he could not refuse: the ambassadorship to Ireland and the Holy See.

Gair grabbed it. But the plan depended on Gair having resigned from the Senate by the time the writs for the election were issued, and when the news inevitably leaked – Dublin was unhappy with, even insulted by, the proposed appointment, and its Canberra embassy passed the news on – Doug Anthony, the Country Party leader, got in touch with the Queensland premier, Joh Bjelke-Petersen, to urge him to get his state governor, Sir Colin Hannah, to issue the writs for an election for five Senate seats forthwith.

Meanwhile, Gair had to be kept from handing in his resignation; he was diverted to the office of a fellow Queensland senator, Ron Maunsell, for what became known as 'The Night of the Long Prawns'. Maunsell and others plied him with beer, whisky and prawns hastily flown in from Brisbane; he was even dragged into the Senate to vote at one point during the evening, so that there could be no question of making his resignation retrospective. The writs were issued; Whitlam, on hearing the news, bellowed, 'Get me Murphy,' and one of the more memorable confrontations between the two leaders took place.

But there was nothing anyone could do about it. Gair later claimed that he had been perfectly aware of why he was being duchessed in Maunsell's office; this may or may not have been the case, but in the prevailing atmosphere, it was plausible; just about anything was.

The next evening, Labor's Barry Cohen and the DLP's Jack Little ended up at the same table in the parliamentary dining room; Little opined that Gair was losing his grip on reality.

Cohen just looked at him. 'Losing his grip?' he eventually spluttered. 'Losing his grip? He's wrecked my party, he's wrecked your party, and now he's going to Dublin on $20,000 a year … and he's the one losing his grip?'

As it turned out, Gair's time in Dublin was neither a long one nor a happy one. He caused an international incident by referring to the British ambassador as an old bugger, and a local one when many of the embassy's female staff resigned, complaining about how he had handled them (literally). When the government changed in 1975, one of its first acts was to recall Gair and give the job to a professional; Gair, the new foreign minister, Andrew Peacock, announced tactfully, was not temperamentally suited to diplomacy. Gair returned to Australia and lived out his final years in well-lubricated obscurity.

But he had left his mark. Towards the end of his prime ministership, Whitlam lamented, 'The Senate will be my pyre.' Vince Gair was surely one of the larger and more combustible logs that made it up.

JOH BJELKE-PETERSEN

S OME TIME IN THE MID-'70S, WHEN JOH BJELKE-PETERSEN was at the height of his powers, I found myself in a bar on Heron Island, off the Queensland coast from Gladstone. Also at the bar were a Queenslander and a Sydneysider, engaged in a frank and fruitful discussion of the Sunshine State and its ruler.

The Sydney man listed an impressive catalogue of mismanagement, cronyism and corruption as the local brooded over his Four-X. Finally, the banana bender replied: 'Well, you can say what you like about Joh, but he's done a hell of a lot for Queensland.'

His exasperated companion snapped back: 'He's done a hell of a lot for himself and his mates, too.'

Not in the least abashed, the Queenslander nodded judiciously. 'Yes,' he drawled. 'That's true. But the way I look at it, if a man's smart enough to get to be premier, he deserves to pull down a bit on the side as well.'

It was then that I realised that Queensland was indeed different, and just how alien Joh had made it.

As the man on Heron Island made clear, Queenslanders not only tolerated the more outrageous aspects of Joh's reign, they positively rejoiced in them. Every murmur of criticism, contempt or downright disbelief from south of the Tweed only confirmed their unique status.

When Gough Whitlam railed against their man as a bible-bashing bastard or simply as a pissant, Queenslanders knew they were on a winner. The general attitude could be summed up as: 'Yes, he may be a criminal lunatic, but he's our criminal lunatic.'

To southerners who saw him only on television, he seemed an immense, towering presence looming over the state he ruled with an iron fist in a tungsten glove. The cartoonist Peter Nicholson used to draw him as a towering Frankenstein's monster, complete with the bolt through the neck.

Thus, I was surprised when I first saw him in the flesh: he was, like other great dictators (Julius Caesar, Napoleon Bonaparte, Bob Hawke) quite a short man, wiry and twitchy rather than lurching and frightening. He exuded energy and a curious kind of magnetism: you knew what he was saying was gibberish and what he was doing was crazy, but you remained fascinated.

A colleague once said that he had eyes like Adolf Eichmann; they were certainly piercing, almost hypnotic, and utterly ruthless. This was, of course, the Christian who crusaded under the slogan: 'Do unto others what they would do unto you – but do it first.'

In the end, the bible-bashing bastard comfortably out-lasted Whitlam and indeed contributed substantially to his defeat. It was Joh's government that frustrated Whitlam's 1974 plan to gain control of the Senate by offering Vince Gair a diplomatic posting. Joh called the election before Gair had formally resigned, and Labor remained one senator short of the numbers it needed.

And more crucially, when the Labor senator Bert Millner died in office in 1975, Joh defied convention by rejecting Labor's nomination to fill the vacancy and appointing his own man, one Patrick Albert Field, with instructions to vote against Labor and give Malcolm Fraser the extra vote he needed to block supply. Hence the constitutional crisis, the dismissal, and the Fraser government.

For a small man, Joh cast a long shadow. Not only did he dominate Queensland, which he treated as a country in its own right. His dismissal of federation was summed up in his dictum: 'There is no such place as Australia. I am the premier of the sovereign state of Queensland and I know whereof I speak.'

A decade later, otherwise sane people such as John Stone, Ian McLachlan and even Andrew Peacock were all at one time or another caught up in the farcical 'Joh for Canberra' movement, launched under the slogan: 'I am determined to turn politics upside down in Australia. I am Joh Bjelke-Petersen of Queensland with a lot of experience and I know what I am doing.'

In the course of his campaign, he wreaked untold damage on the world at large. At its start, he was able to reveal that there were only forty-two free countries on the face of the earth; a week later the number had fallen to twenty-four, no fewer than eighteen democracies having fallen to what he called 'communist Idi Amins' in the space of seven days.

But if he finally spluttered out of the federal scene, his control in Queensland remained unchallengeable; not only did he see off a platoon of Labor leaders with names like Perc (sic) Tucker, but he ripped his alleged allies in the Liberal Party to shreds in the process.

And even when he lost out to Canberra, as in the banning of sand mining on Fraser Island or control of the Great Barrier Reef, he could parlay it into a kind of victory. 'I don't know what all the fuss is about,' he once scoffed of the reef. 'I've been out to see the coral myself and there's no sign of damage, it's all beautifully clean and white.' As, indeed, he saw the whole of Queensland – from a rather different perspective than that of the Fitzgerald Report.

The Joh era was both ugly and bizarre, but there are a couple of things to be learned from it. First, it may be all right to appropriate New Zealander movie stars, sportsmen and race-horses, but leave the politicians alone or it will end in tears. And second, beware of electing stop-gap leaders: they can outstay their welcome until they think they are indispensable.

JOHN KERR

GOUGH WHITLAM WAS NEVER A GREAT ONE FOR admitting that he had got it wrong – not before, during or after his time as prime minister. But even he was forced to acknowledge that his appointment of Sir John Kerr as governor-general could have turned out better. Not that it was his fault; he had, as always, behaved impeccably. He had been betrayed in the most base and deceitful fashion, but how could he have predicted it?

Kerr's credentials were there for all to see. A working-class boy from Balmain, he had been a protégé of the great Doc Evatt; he had stood for Labor preselection in 1951. He had defended *Oz* magazine against the wowsers of the day. He was a former chief justice of New South Wales and had run the inquiry that set up the Remuneration Tribunal, which determined MPs' pay and conditions. And he was a mate of such Labor luminaries as Neville Wran, Jim McClelland and Joe Riordan. What could possibly go wrong?

Well, where to begin? Kerr had formally resigned from the ALP in 1956, and although he never actually joined the breakaway DLP, he had certainly veered towards it. In 1969, as a judge of the Industrial Court, he had jailed the trade unionist Clarrie O'Shea for refusing to pay a court-imposed fine. It could be argued that, under the law of the time, Kerr had little choice, but there were those who felt he had shown unnecessary relish for the task.

Then there was the CIA connection: during the Second World War, Kerr had worked for Australian intelligence, liaising closely with the Americans, and in the 1950s he joined the Association for Cultural Freedom, a front organisation established and financed by the CIA to fight communist influence in developing countries, of which Australia was then judged to be one. In 1966 he became the first chairman of LawAsia, another CIA affiliate. The CIA, of course, regarded the Whitlam government as an enemy, especially for its opposition to the Vietnam conflict.

Over the years Kerr had moved well to the right, and now counted Sir Garfield Barwick – chief justice of the High Court and a former minister in the Menzies government – among his closest confidants. If he ever had been a trustworthy Labor ally, he certainly wasn't anymore. Margaret Whitlam distrusted him from the start. She had been a close friend of Kerr's first wife, Peggy, and was disturbed by the fact that within months of her death, Kerr married the ex-wife of a colleague, Hugh Robson. Kerr's fellow judges had facilitated a quickie divorce for 'Fancy Nancy', as she was known in legal circles; she had acted as his interpreter in Hawaii during the war years. The first Hugh Robson knew of his former wife's speedy remarriage was when he was informed of it by his son. It was a minor scandal at the time and should perhaps have warned Whitlam that Kerr was not quite as punctilious and scrupulous as he appeared. But by then it was too late; the new viceroy was firmly ensconced in Yarralumla.

To be fair, he was not Whitlam's first choice. The prime minister would have been perfectly happy to have let Sir Paul Hasluck continue in the role; by then he had made his peace with his old political foe and trusted him to act according to convention. But Hasluck had had enough and wanted to get out of politics altogether. Then Whitlam turned to Kenneth Myer, a widely respected Melbourne businessman. Myer too declined. By now it was known that the job would shortly become vacant, and the prime minister's office was bombarded with suggestions from all sides. My own was the poet and conservationist Judith Wright. Whitlam was attracted to the idea; appointing Australia's first woman GG, and a prominent figure in the arts at that, appealed to his sense of the dramatic.

But more cautious counsellors prevailed, and eventually Whitlam settled for what he believed was the conservative option: Sir John Robert Kerr, AK, GCMG, GCVO, QC. The establishment was happy; some of Whitlam's Labor colleagues, who knew a little of the man's background, were rather less so.

Initially things went smoothly enough. Kerr granted Whitlam the double dissolution of 1974 and convened the joint sitting of parliament that followed. But soon after that, the blunders surrounding the loans affair began to emerge, and Kerr, we know now, became both concerned and annoyed – more, it appears, because he had been left out of the decision-making than through concern about any impropriety. The conservatives began to apply pressure; he was, they said, being taken for granted, treated with contempt. His new wife Nancy was enlisted to help.

Kerr had always been a big drinker; before his appointment his sessions with Lionel Murphy, among others, had been legendary. One long lunch at the Lobby restaurant in Canberra ended with Kerr sliding happily under the table, to be retrieved by his long-suffering driver. It soon became clear that just because Kerr had been appointed as the Queen's representative, he was not about to break the habit of a lifetime. On one occasion, the Kerrs were in residence at Admiralty House in Sydney, with the Whitlams next door at Kirribilli House. One night, as the prime minister's staff were working late in the living room, they were startled to hear an insistent tapping on the French windows. It was their neighbour, in desperate search of whisky; he had apparently drunk the available supplies in Admiralty House dry.

At this stage, such incidents remained at least semi-private; it was a couple of years before Kerr was to astonish the nation with his slapstick performance presenting the prizes at the 1977 Melbourne Cup. But the fact that they occurred at all should have warned Whitlam that his safe and conservative appointment was becoming a shade unpredictable.

The signs worsened after Malcolm Fraser blocked supply in 1975. Most of the Labor Party were simply puzzled; surely the opposition leader must realise that he was on a hiding to nothing. Whitlam was not going to crack. But some of the calmer heads were worried: Fraser was a ruthless operator, but not normally a reckless one. Did he know something they didn't? And could it, just possibly, involve Whitlam's man in Yarralumla? As the crisis deepened, so did their concerns. After one meeting with Kerr, Bill Hayden rang Whitlam in something close to panic. 'My copper's instinct tells me the bastard's going to sack us,' he warned bluntly.

But Whitlam dismissed the fear: Kerr was both too bound by convention and too weak. 'He wouldn't dare,' the prime minister replied confidently. But this was in fact the very weakness Fraser had identified and was playing on: Kerr's personal insecurity was his vulnerable spot. With just one decision, he could go down in history as the man who redeemed Australia, Fraser and his ministers kept cajoling him. And they encouraged him to a preliminary breach with convention: Whitlam had specifically instructed the viceroy to seek advice only from the elected government, but Kerr consulted his old friend Sir Garfield Barwick, who, unsurprisingly, told him he had both the right and the duty to act. This advice was confirmed by another conservative High Court judge, Sir Anthony Mason.

So Kerr had one last stiff drink and jumped off the cliff, taking both the government and the constitution with him. To compound the offence, he refused to accept a message from the speaker of the house, Gordon Scholes, informing him that the House of Representatives had voted no confidence in Fraser and wanted him to recommission Whitlam as prime minister. Kerr then summarily prorogued the parliament. With one stroke he had undone nearly three centuries of the democratic political evolution of the Westminster system of government.

Whitlam proclaimed, 'Nothing will save the governorgeneral.' But the immediate public response was the reverse. The electorate had been growing increasingly uneasy about Whitlam and his government; now, it appeared, all their worst fears had been confirmed. He must have done something terrible; they didn't know what it was, but for the Queen's representative, the governor-general Whitlam himself had appointed, to have sacked him, it must have been horrendous. They voted Whitlam out in a landslide and repeated the treatment in 1977. The nation was deeply and bitterly divided, but for the first few years Kerr had the numbers. He increased his drinking and cut down on his public appearances, which were frequently beset by demonstrators. On one of these occasions I described the viceroy as 'a wellmarinated blood plum, topped with cheap yoghurt'.

When his term ran out at the end of 1977, Fraser attempted to give him one last reward by naming him as Australia's ambassador to UNESCO, a comfortable post based in Paris. But, coming as it did so soon after the national embarrassment of the Melbourne Cup, this was a step too far. Amid public outcry, the appointment was cancelled. Ironically, ten years later Bob Hawke gave the job to Gough Whitlam, who filled it with panache.

Kerr disappeared from the public scene and soon after moved to London, where he saw out his days in the well-lubricated ambience of various gentlemen's clubs. He died in 1991. Whitlam comfortably outlasted his nemesis, both in longevity and latterly in public esteem. But Fraser's flattering forecast was at least half-right: Sir John Kerr has indeed gone down in history.

EPILOGUE

'It was the best of times, it was the worst of times . . .'

CHARLES DICKENS

THE SOCIAL REALIST WAS WRITING OF THE FRENCH Revolution some fifty years after the Romantic poet with which we began, and he was far more equivocal about it. And so it is with the Whitlam government: more than a generation has passed, but a definitive judgement has still not emerged.

There are those who revere those brief three years as the Australian renaissance, a period of reform unequalled before or since, a time of vision, courage and panache that stands in stark contrast to the shallow, poll-driven politics of today. And there are others who use those years as a cautionary tale to scare the voters with accounts of economic vandalism, ministerial excess and a political hubris that brought the country to the edge of disaster. The only common ground between the two is that with Gough Whitlam, you always knew where you stood: he went to inordinate lengths to explain his program well in advance, so that while his opponents may have hated everything he stood for, they could hardly claim to be surprised when he went about implementing it.

Forty years later, the survivors of the Whitlam mob remain unapologetic; while not all have obeyed their leader's injunction to maintain the rage, and most will now admit that his government had its blemishes (to adopt the euphemism John Howard used to refer to the crimes committed against Indigenous Australians), few will argue that the shake-up was not necessary; nearly all agree that after twenty-three years of conservative rule, it was indeed time for changes, most of which were long overdue. And if it ended in tears, most of them were due to the refusal of the government's opponents to accept its right to govern, and the devious, unscrupulous and convention-smashing tactics they used to bring it down.

I, for one, am not ashamed to say that I miss those days of roller-coaster politics, when every day was an unprecedented trapeze act performed without a safety net, when the future was a joyful challenge rather than a gloomy threat, and anything appeared possible in a world of hope and promise. It was not all bliss; it was certainly not relaxed and comfortable. But it was a wonderful thing to be part of.

Let us finish with yet another visit to the French Revolution. It is reported that when Whitlam first visited China in 1971, he had a long audience with China's eminent and erudite premier, Chou En-lai. In the course of a wide-ranging discussion, he asked Chou his views about the events of 1789 and their aftermath; could the revolution be accounted a success? Chou pondered for a moment and then replied: 'It's too early to say.'

It has since been suggested that Chou had misunderstood the question and thought Whitlam was referring to the Chinese revolution of 1949, or even the Cultural Revolution which followed it. But whatever the truth, the great statesman's warning about the need for caution before making unequivocal judgements stands.

History will eventually pronounce its verdict on the Whitlam mob and their opponents. But even today we can say one thing with certainty: they were a pretty wild and colourful bunch. And a hell of a lot more fun than the present lot, both to be around and to write about.

© PETER NICHOLSON

www.ingramcontent.com/pod-product-compliance
Lightning Source LLC
Chambersburg PA
CBHW050351270326
41926CB00016B/3698